FAITH IN TRIBULATION

The  Show
Volume Four

Episodes 31 through 40

Julie Rowe and Eric J. Smith

ISBN: 9781672011266

Cover design by Eric J. Smith; *photo acquired:*
https://wallpaperbetter.com

Printed in the United States of America

To listen to the Julie Rowe Show, please visit:
http://www.youtube.com/c/JulieRoweShow

Other Related Sites:
http://julieroweprepare.com
https://doctrinalessays.com

TABLE OF CONTENTS

ACKNOWLEDGMENTS

Julie and Eric wish to thank those who helped transcribe these podcasts. Their dedicated efforts are greatly appreciated. They also express their gratitude to their spouses and children who have made sacrifices to allow these recordings to be completed.

AUTHOR'S NOTE

The original transcripts of these podcasts were carefully prepared by our team of transcriptionists. Nearly every sound made by Julie, Eric, and the guests was included. For the sake of readability and continuity of the text, repetitive phrases have been removed, along with most of the verbal responses that weren't tied directly to the message.

In other words, this book series is not intended to be a "read along" with the podcasts. Some of the paragraphs have been tightened up to make Julie's message more concise. Also, long segments of dialogue have been divided into paragraphs where it was appropriate, and in some cases, run-on sentences that are characteristic of live conversation were turned into complete sentences.

Julie and Eric appreciate hearing from their listeners and supporters. They may be reached individually or together at agreatertomorrow2014@gmail.com. To listen to the podcasts, visit The Julie Rowe Show at http://www.youtube.com/c/JulieRoweShow

Jewish Holidays
and Heavenly Signs

Julie: Welcome to the Julie Rowe Show. Today is Tuesday, August 29, 2017. Today, Eric and I have a topic that has been on my mind quite a bit the last several weeks and so I'm going to turn the time over to Eric and have him introduce the topic today.

Eric: Thanks Julie. We've been talking a lot about signs in the heavens and Jewish holidays but we've only touched on those topics just lightly, really; there's so much more that could be said. Julie has been explaining to me that she's had more impressions even after what's already been said, and she'd like to talk about that more.

I want to just start by introducing the idea of Jewish traditions and holidays and so forth. I'm not by any means an expert in this area, but I wanted to say that I have studied Hebrew quite a bit and I've really enjoyed learning the language and studying it. I'd like to just share some of my enthusiasm with you about Jewish traditions, and Hebrew.

It's always so uplifting to me to research words. The thing I love about Hebrew and Jewish traditions is: *everything* has meaning. You can take just the simple Hebrew alphabet and each letter in that alphabet has significance and meaning, unlike in the English alphabet, where a letter is simply just a letter. So I want to give a little example of why I love Hebrew so much. There's a great word for truth, and a little historical sketch about the word truth in Hebrew. As I was saying each letter has meaning in Hebrew. The first letter is

Alef, which is "A", and this letter has meaning. It's also the number one; it also means God; it means the beginning; it can mean past.

The middle letter of the alphabet is Mem or "M" and it means present. It has lots of meanings. The last letter in the alphabet is like our T, it's *Tav*. And so that can mean things in the future. If you combine the letters A, M, and T in Hebrew it makes the word AMET, which is the word for truth. Truth can be defined as: things as they were things as they are and things as they will be. And so, you can see how the combination of those three letters the A, M, and T came together and created this word.

Everything has meaning and to Jews and Israelites, even today, everything has meaning. Days have meaning and relationships. I love the way they celebrate. They have feasts for things. And I've noticed in our own culture, American culture especially, is a tendency for our holidays to be geared towards, well, and I don't mean this in any disrespect, but we kind of self aggrandize. We tend to suit our self gratification. We gorge ourselves with cake and candy and all these things but in Jewish and in Hebrew/Israeli culture, it's kind of the opposite. Holidays usually have a focus on God and instead of turning inward they turn outward to celebrate things and give back to the community, and donate to charities, and focus on their relationships with others and with God and this one of the things I love the very most about Jewish culture.

So with all that said, there are a number of holidays and other things that Julie and I'll discuss a little today and I'll turn the time back to you Julie and see what comes to your mind.

Julie: Great, thank you for sharing that Eric. First I want to let people know that I am by no means an expert in Jewish holiday or tradition. I have been told and shown that I am a descendant on the Davidic line of Jewish ancestry from Judah as well as going back to Joseph and the house of Ephraim. That is my lineage so I think this one of the reasons the Spirit's been prompting me to learn a little bit about the Jewish traditions and cultures and holidays but also because it does tie in very specifically to my mission and to what we have going on in the universe right now, specifically related to the time of year that we're in having just passed the solar eclipse on August 21st of 2017 and anticipating that we're going to have the planets aligning on September 23rd.

As we see the Book of Revelation written by John the Revelator coming into fulfillment from 2016 to 2017. So I wanted to start out with Rosh Hashanah, which is the Jewish New Year. Some of this I'm just going to be reading off of the internet and other sources; mostly Wikipedia, which you guys can look up and if you haven't I encourage you to look up. Now we know not everything's correct on Wikipedia so if I get this wrong that just shows my ignorance related to the Jewish traditions of holidays, but I'm doing the best I can to follow the Spirit on this and just at least give people a basic exposure and then you can do your own research.

Interestingly enough, just in the last week we've had a few different emails come in from individuals who have listened to the podcasts and they themselves have put timelines and other things together of these holidays and so we may be quoting from some of those as well. Rosh Hashanah, which is the Jewish New Year is a season that's considered a time for repentance and in Jewish tradition they have specific prayers, or penitential prayers, which are repentance prayers, that are called *Selichot* that are added to the daily prayers except for on Shabbat. And so these prayers are done each weekday during what they call the month of Elul - how do you say it Eric? Eric's a lot better at Hebrew tradition. How do you pronounce that?

Eric: You know it probably doesn't matter too much but I would probably say "eh-lewl".

Julie: Elul. And so these prayers are recited and on the eve of the first day, being the 29th, and Rosh Hashanah the one to two, tishrei or tishri according to oral tradition. This is the head of the year, or the day of memorial or repentance, and the Day of Judgment that comes. So what they talk about in this tradition is that God appears in the role of a king, remembering and judging each person individually according to his or her deeds, and making a decree for each person for the following year.

So this new year is just starting and we're looking at the end of last year ending with an end of Jubilee and then coming into a new year with Yom Kippur, being another holiday that will be recognized and we'll talk about that in a minute, but Rosh Hashanah is a holiday characterized by one specific Mitzvah, and the blowing of the shofar - and a shofar is a type of horn if you will. According to the Torah, which is the book of scripture used by the Jews, it's the first day of the seventh month of the calendar year and they have their own calendar years, they don't go by the calendars that the rest of us use here in America. This marks the beginning of a ten-day period leading up to Yom Kippur, so that the ten day period from Rosh Hashanah to Yom Kippur, and according to two of the Talmudic opinions, the creation of the world was completed on Rosh Hashanah.

So there's significance in that with the meaning as far as tradition goes. They have morning prayer services, they talk about the majesty and judgments of God, remembrance the birth of the world, and then the blowing of the shofar. The Bible specifies that Rosh Hashanah as a one-day holiday but it's traditionally celebrated two days, even within the land of Israel, and the Torah, apparently, does not use any term like "New Year" in reference to Rosh Hashanah; it specifies four different New Year's days for different purposes, and the first one being, I don't know how to say Tishrei, which is the conventional Rosh Hashanah or new year for calculating calendar years or sabbatical year, the Shemitah, and the Jubilee, or the cycles and the age of the trees for purposes of Jewish law and they're for separating grains and tithes.

This goes into the references we've made before about balances of scales and finances and other things on a grander scale with what's going on in the world and in the United States. Then the Shabbat, or New Year for trees, and their current agricultural cycle, that's related to tithes so this also goes into play with agriculture which can affect things on a spiritual level like famines and droughts.

Then the Nisan New Year, for counting months and major festivals and for calculating the years of the reign of a Jewish King. In Biblical times, the day following 29 Adar, the year of the reign of the King would be followed by one Nisan or year two of the reign of the king or a certain individual, and in modern times, although the Jewish calendar year numbers changes on Rosh Hashanah, the months are still numbered for Nisan. So it gets a little bit confusing to those of us here in the West that don't follow this.

There are three pilgrimage festivals that are always reckoned as coming in the order of Passover and if, I don't know how to say this either, Shabbat or Shabbat Sukkot, and it can have religious law consequences even in modern times. And the Elul, which is a year for animal tithes. So they talk about another one with the ten days of repentance, and with the ten days of repentance during that time, this all in anticipation of Yom Kippur and Yom Kippur is huge. In these ten days they examine their deeds and they repent for the sins that they've committed against God and other people, and it can take on the form of additional supplications, confessing one's deeds before God, fasting, self-reflection, and an increase in involvement with or donations to charity. Do you have anything to say about that Eric? Want to add anything?

Eric: No, not necessarily. I think you're covering it really well.

Julie: Okay. So Yom Kippur which is considered Day of Atonement; that's the holiest day of the year for Jews and its central theme is atonement and reconciliation. This accomplished through prayer and fasting; including abstinence from all food and drink, including water by all healthy adults, bathing, wearing of perfume or cologne, wearing of leather shoes, and sexual relations are some of the other prohibitions on Yom Kippur and all of them are designed to ensure that the individual's attention is completely and absolutely focused on the quest for atonement with God.

So Yom Kippur is also unique among holidays having work-related restrictions identical to those of Shabbat. And so the fast and other prohibitions commence on the tenth day at sunset, with sunset being the beginning of the day in Jewish tradition. So they reverse it; sunset is their beginning of their day, unlike our sunrise. They have a prayer that's traditionally recited just before sunset, although it's often regarded as the start of Yom Kippur evening service. It's technically a separate tradition. So they recite this prayer at sunset and then it's actually recited on the ninth day, which is the day before Yom Kippur, and it's not recited on Yom Kippur itself which is the tenth day, which begins after sunset. And you can look up more about that and the difference between those prayers and what they mean.

They also have a four-cornered prayer shawl which is worn for evening and afternoon prayers, the only day of the year in which this done. And again, I encourage you to look up some of that tradition. If you were to study it out in biblical times, there are references in the Bible regarding some of these prayers and prayer shawls and things like that. So, the services in all the traditions are the longest of the year on Yom Kippur and in some traditional synagogues prayers run continuously from morning until nightfall, or nearly so.

For their prayer of remembrance, they will quote poems and other temple services that take place on Yom Kippur. Yom Kippur is so huge that basically, my understanding is at the end of Yom Kippur then the judgments of God come. And so if one were to look at this from Western culture we could basically say "okay, we've had this eclipse, we're going to have the planets aligning, we're going to have Rosh Hashanah starting, and then Yom Kippur, which is repentance hopefully being completed, and anything or anyone who has not repented at that point in time will suffer the judgments of God. Do you have anything to add on that?

Eric: Nope. You're nailing it.

Julie: Okay, (laughs). So, Yom Kippur is considered, along with the 15th of Av, as the happiest days of the year. And I love that! I think it's amazing right?! A lot of people associate with repentance; with something sad like God is a mean God who's making people do what He wants but I know, and I testify, that the atonement is for us, and it's a gift, and repentance is a gift of God for us. It helps lighten our hearts and it helps us turn to Him as He carries our burdens. And that's really what repentance is about. So I love that they celebrate in this manner.

The other thing is: Sukkot, which is feast of booths or tabernacles. The Feast of Tabernacles, which is also coming up. Now in 2017 this was coming up in October, the first week of October in 2018, this will actually occur the same week that these planets are aligning this year between the 23rd, and the 30th of September will be Sukkot next year, and so that's significant as well. We will have the 14th anniversary of my near-death experience and significant changes next year during this week of Sukkot. This specific holiday is a seven-day festival which is known also as a Feast of the Booths, or a Feast of Tabernacles, or just Tabernacles. It's one of three pilgrimage festivals mentioned in the Bible. So this huge. This goes back generations and generations.

The Sukkot commemorates the years that the Jews spent in the desert on their way to the Promised Land celebrates the way in which God protected them under difficult desert conditions. The word Sukkot is the plural of the Hebrew word sukkah meaning: booth. Jews are commanded to dwell in booths during the holidays. And this usually means taking, you know, some sleep in it but, but not all of them but especially in Israel. There are specific rules for constructing those sukkah and then it goes into some of the traditions there which I've been shown, symbolically speaking, some of these. I did not realize on a conscious level but this was what Sukkot was about.

I was shown this in dream and visions of the significance of palm leaves, willow, and what they call the citron. And that goes into play with this holiday and I just learned that in the last week and a half. This what it says related to that: It's a ritual; unique holiday is the use of four species; the palm, the myrtle, the willow, and the citron. On each day of the holiday, other than Shabbat, these are waved in association with the recitation of hallel in the synagogue. Then walks in a procession around the synagogue called Hoshaanot. And on the seventh day of the Sukkot is called Hoshanah Rabbah, the great Hashanah, singular Hoshanah and the source of the English word Hosanna. I think that's just amazing when we get to the root word, and then the root tradition, of something like the Hosanna Shout or even songs that are popular where we hear people praising Jesus Christ, or praising the Lord, with the word Hosanna.

That's representative of the palm, the myrtle, the willow, and the citron. Then they have different prayers and processions. The tradition mimics practices from the temple in Jerusalem and many aspects of the customs also resemble those of Rosh Hashanah and Yom Kippur. Rosh Hashanah Rabbah is traditionally taken to be the day of delivery of the final judgment of the Yom Kippur, and offers the last opportunity for pleas of repentance before the holiday season closes. And I find that interesting, too, that we have first Rosh Hashanah which is the new year, then we have Yom Kippur which is repentance, and then you have this other Sukkot and the Hashanah Rabah, which gives people an opportunity for a last opportunity to plea for repentance before the holiday closes and judgment comes. Do you have anything to add about that Eric?

Eric: No, but can you bring it home for us now? You've just mentioned a whole bunch of holidays then. What does that mean? How does that overlay with our times?

Julie: Well the first thing that comes to my mind is kind of the same thing everybody else was wondering is: when is this earthquake in Utah going to happen? (Laughs) Right?

Eric: (Laughs) Right.

Julie: We're like: "we all feel it getting closer". None of us knows exactly when it's going to come. If we've got Yom Kippur coming, in less than 40 days now and we have the planets aligning, fulfilling the Book of Revelation coming on September 23rd. We have Days of Repentance and pleading but we know through revelation that the majority of the earth will *not* be repenting and therefore we know that judgment will come. I do know this; we are *not* having an earthquake before Yom Kippur finishes. After that, all bets are off. People have asked me when the earthquake is. I said "I don't know". I know when it's *not* and I know it's not going to happen in September but after that, I really don't know. I think it'll be interesting to find out how soon after we finish Yom Kippur we have that earthquake.

Eric: Interesting. You know Julie, in our culture there's a lot of fear. We've talked a lot about fear energy surrounding signs in the heavens, and I think it's become sort of a taboo topic to talk about eclipses and things happening in the heavens.

Julie: Right. Like you're some kind of weird mystic if you get involved in it. You know?

Eric: Right, right. The Bible talks about soothsayers and there are cultures and religions that sort of base their philosophies upon things in the heavens but I want to just point out how scriptural it really is. Of course to the Hebrews, their calendar system was based off a lunar calendar.

Julie: Mm hmm.

Eric: Here in the Gregorian system in modern times, we base it off the Sun mostly. And so that's why a lot of these eclipses that have happened in previous years have always fallen on Jewish holidays. I find that really interesting.

Julie: Right

Eric: I think it's also worth mentioning you don't have to look farther than Genesis chapter 1 verse 14 for the purpose of signs: *And God said, Let there be lights in the firmament of the heaven to divide the day from the night; and let them be for signs, and for seasons, and for days, and years.*

Julie: Mm hmm.

Eric: So one of the very purposes that He created stars and things in the heavens was for signs.

Julie: I agree.

Eric: There are a number of other scriptures, and I think it's important that we establish that we actually *should* be watching for the signs. I see in people's emails sometimes and comments who'll say: "I'm not trying to watch for signs or anything..." But here's the thing; we *should* be watching for signs. Doctrine & Covenants section 88 says: *and unto you shall be given to know the signs of the times and the signs of the coming of the Son of Man.* 1st Thessalonians 5:1-6; I just want to read this, it's a couple of verses long but worth reading:

> "*But of the times and the seasons, brethren, ye have no need that I write unto you. For yourselves know perfectly that the day of the Lord so cometh as a thief in the night. For when they shall say, Peace and safety; then sudden destruction cometh upon them, as travail upon a woman with child; and they shall not escape. But ye, brethren, are not in darkness, that that day should overtake you as a thief. Ye are all the children of light, and the children of the day: we are not of the night, nor of darkness. Therefore let us not sleep, as do others; but let us watch and be sober.*"

Doctrine and Covenants 45 takes it further and says: *"Even so it shall be in that day when they shall see all these things, then shall they know that the hour is nigh. And it shall come to pass that he that feareth me shall be looking forth for the great day of the Lord to come, even for the signs of the coming of the Son of Man. And they shall see signs and wonders, for they shall be shown forth in the heavens above, and in the earth beneath.*

Julie: Thank You.

Eric: Yeah, yeah you're welcome. There are just a few scriptures that shed light on this need that we actually have to watch for the signs, and that those things that happen in the heavens are an indication that the time is drawing near for the Son of God to come back to the world.

Julie: That's excellent. I appreciate you sharing that Eric. It brings my mind again to some of the signs in the heavens that we're talking about here with the traditions and the Book of Revelation. I'd like to talk about that a little bit more.

Revelation 12. And I'm just going to quote a portion of that. We've done it before I want to do it again with this, and then I'm going to give you just *one* interpretation. It has layered meaning. Now I've come across different interpretations of Revelation 12, and I need to let you know that those on the other side of the veil have let me know that this interpretation of Revelation is just *one of many*. It's extremely layered and there is more to it than this but I want you to listen to what the Spirit tells you about this, and see if you could pick up on the hidden or deeper meanings that are not just what I'm saying with my mouth but what the Spirit's teaching you as we talk about both my mission and those that have been foreordained to participate in the gathering.

Revelation 12: 1-2: *"And there appeared a great wonder in heaven; a woman clothed with the sun, and the moon under her feet, and upon her head a crown of twelve stars: And she being with child cried, travailing in birth, and pained to be delivered."* On September 23rd there are going to be two constellations, Virgo and Leo that are going to line up with Leo above Virgo. Normally Leo only has nine stars but on *that* night Mercury, Mars, and Venus will roll in and line up with the other stars above Virgo which will present twelve stars, which is symbolic of the twelve stars around the crown.

The moon will be at the feet of the constellation and Virgo will be clothed with the Sun. So, the constellation Virgo, meaning "the virgin", the twelve stars represents in one meaning, the twelve stars represent the twelve tribes of Israel. It represents the bride, or the Church of God which represents Christ, and it has nine stars until September 23rd as Mercury, Mars, the constellation Leo, the lion represents the tribe of Judah. Its brightest star is Regulus, and Venus lines up and moves into the constellation and makes 12 stars. On this date it is above the constellation of Virgo. I have been told specifically that my mission ties in *directly* to this planet alignment. Just pay attention to that as time goes on. As you see more, revealed both about my mission and *the Mission* regarding the gathering, and the Lord bringing His children home.

In Revelation 12 again it says: *"And she brought forth a man child, who was to rule all nations with a rod of iron: and her child was caught up unto God, and to his throne."* Also that day, on September 23rd, Jupiter, the king planet, will begin to move down between the legs of Virgo where it has been since December 18th of 2016, around nine months.

And then again in Revelation 12 it says: *"And there appeared another wonder in heaven; and behold a great red dragon, having seven heads and ten horns, and seven crowns upon his heads. And his tail drew the third part of the stars of heaven, and did cast them to the earth: and the dragon stood before the woman which was ready to be delivered, for to devour her child as soon as it was born."* So this both symbolic and literal when we're talking about the woman in travail. And in reference to the Church and to what those stars represent, including the 12 tribes of Israel and the gathering. My mission is directly tied to, essentially being, like, a poster child for the gathering.

I'm not even going into more detail on that right now but I want you to pay attention. Study up in the scriptures, in Revelation 12 because we are seeing this come of fulfillment as we speak. Eric do you have anything to add to that?

Eric: I don't, but I think there's a lot on the internet concerning the constellations; everything you just described with the woman and the way stars are moving and things. I really do think that John the Revelator had full awareness of the constellations and the way those stars would move and I think he was describing those things literally. I know that there are other symbols as well in there and so, like Julie said, it is layered. There's a lot we can derive in reading these verses.

Julie: Right.

Eric: There's that part where it spoke of the War in Heaven and Michael and the dragon and these things. We often read that as a premortal experience and it certainly was - again, this layered - but if you study that, you may find that there's actually meaning to the future as well.

Julie: I agree.

Eric: Again, one of those dual meanings.

Julie: I agree. When I was shown past, present, future and I recently came out publicly letting people know in the podcast that I report to John the Revelator, who actually wrote the Book of Revelation. It makes sense doesn't it? That is John, who is my distant ancestor, as I am a descendant on the Davidic line, and that they would assign John to oversee my mission because essentially it's his mission.

Eric: Right

Julie: I'm just one of many people that will help him fulfill his mission as John wrote this Book, he was shown past, present, future and he wrote in a layered manner so that he was speaking both of past, present, and future which is why it's so layered and that's difficult for a lot of people to get the meaning. What's going on, again in Revelation chapter 12:6: "*And the woman fled into the wilderness, where she hath a place prepared of God, that they should feed her there a thousand two hundred and threescore days.*"

After Christ's apostles in the ancient church were martyred the church eventually went into apostasy and the Church of God was taken from the Earth. The church of the devil was entrenched and many plain and precious truths were taken from the Bible and we're going to see that happen again. There will be those who apostatize from the church. There will be those who will be martyred, and there will be those who will then go as the remnant from the Church of Jesus Christ of Latter- day Saints, and remnants of other seed that will come together with the tribes of Israel bringing the twelve tribes of Israel back together, to begin the Church of the Firstborn, as 144,000 are called and sent out to do missionary work. Do you have anything to say about that Eric?

Eric: I think verse six that you just read is interesting. I've noticed this pattern in scripture: whenever you see this reference to *a thousand two hundred and threescore days*, if you do the math that's three and a half years. There's an interesting tie-in to Daniel in the Old Testament, who spoke of the abomination of desolation. He had two references, I believe: one in days (maybe it was months), and another reference was in weeks. But when you do the math they each end up being three and a half years as well. Christ, in Matthew, tells us about the Desolation of Abomination that Daniel spoke of. And, they refer to a time period of tribulation, and when you put those two together that it's all these three-and-a-half-year time periods you know?

Julie: Right

Eric: Anyway, when you put those two periods together you have seven years and so I think that's significant. I think it's also interesting to note that the solar eclipse we just had could very well mark the beginning of that, or close to the beginning of it, and then we'll have another solar eclipse in seven years.

Julie: I find that fascinating. Something else I find fascinating we're talking about math, and as they've been trying to teach me about my mission. They'd explain to me, essentially, I will be hidden up in the wilderness, or will go to a gathering place in the mountains, for three and a half years before I will experience a change in my body, and then the Tribulations will continue until we reach the seven years. And so I find it interesting that the pattern of three and a half years even applies to my mission with what they're showing me. Whatever that mission is, I don't have a complete picture of it but they are giving me more and more information that I find it fascinating that there is spiritual significance to the three and a half years for many individuals.

Eric: Mm hmm

Julie: Thanks for sharing that Eric. I wanted to talk a little bit about what we have coming up in the world. I've been doing business meetings with GTRF and have made some good contacts. I have been working on some of these funding issues with the documentary and some other things that we're working on with GTRF. We're setting up an aviation company and some other things for rescue missions on human trafficking as we do all this in preparation for the tribulations.

Then going into the next decade or so, I'm absolutely fascinated with how the Lord is orchestrating this work. You know, I'm a middle-aged mom from Kansas. I do have a decent resume on the business side as far as some of the things I've gone through and the Lord helping to prepare me, but by all accounts I should not in any way be qualified to be doing some of what I'm doing, other than that the Lord has qualified me and they're qualifying all the individuals that I'm working with.

I've been able to meet amazing people of every group you can imagine. We have a lot of LDS people; we have people from various faiths across the country; and I'm just *amazed* at the timing of things as they're coming together. I've been working for two years now on GTRF. I started it in August of 2015 and this month, the contacts that I've made and the work that we've been doing is starting to come and pay off and come to fruition.

In September we are going to be seeing some amazing things happening with GTRF, and I'm excited to make some of those announcements as those come to fruition. I know that the Lord is orchestrating this plan. I know that these holidays and these traditions are not coincidental when it comes to what's going on in the world right now. I know that nothing's coincidental regarding what the Lord would have us do to fulfill His promises that He's made to His children.

He fulfills all of His promises. He loves each and every one of us so much that He's giving us these signs in the heavens. He's giving us these different types of education from across cultures to help us get the communications out there to each other as we can warn and testify and help each other no matter where we are in the world.

Although I am not skilled or very educated in Jewish tradition or holiday, there *are* people that really are and they've been sending me some amazing things. I wanted to thank those who've been emailing me with information about this. It kind of helped give me clarity that we need to be paying more and more attention to this, and tying in our research with what current presidents of the church, prophets and apostles are saying in regards to being spiritually prepared; obeying the Sabbath day and continually preparing on a spiritual level.

We can do all the preparations in the world on a physical level but spiritually speaking, if we're not paying attention to the signs in the heavens, if we're not paying attention to what the spirit's telling us, at the end of the day, none of the other stuff's going to matter.

So with that, Eric, I just wanted to thank you for the time that we've had today. I encourage those that are listening to spread this message to others, let them know that we have some big things coming up this fall. We've got Yom Kippur which, whether we're Jewish or not, this applies to us as well because that's how the world works. And, we have Day of Judgment coming very soon. I just wanted to spread my love to those who are listening and encourage you to do the same. Focus on the basics; focus on your family, and turn to God because that's where safety comes from. Eric, thank you so much for your time today.

Eric: Julie, thank you. I appreciate your words. I'd like to just end on a final thought here. I want to express my love for all those who may be listening who have Jewish connections or ancestry. You are children of Judah. You are of the house of Israel. You have a sacred role in the Plan of Salvation. I know God has His watchful eye on you and your people.

I want to read this final thought from Moroni, a prophet in the Book of Mormon. In 3rd Nephi chapter 29 he said, speaking of latter-days: "*Yea, and ye need not any longer hiss, nor spurn, nor make game of the Jews, nor any of the remnant of the house of Israel; for behold, the Lord remembereth his covenant unto them, and he will do unto them according to that which he hath sworn.*"

I leave that and my witness, in the name of Jesus Christ.

Julie: Eric, thank you. I love that scripture. I look forward to working more with my brothers and sisters across the globe and I appreciate those listening today. Thank you for your faith. Thank you for the testimonies. Keep up the good work, until next time.

Tribulations 101

Episode 32

Julie Rowe: Welcome to the Julie Rowe Show. Today is Thursday, August 31, 2017. Today Eric and I have been talking about several different podcast ideas and decided upon one, and I'm going to turn the time over to Eric for him to introduce that for us.

Eric Smith: Sounds good. Thanks, Julie. One of the topics of the latter-days that often comes up, and you've mentioned in your books, is the tribulations. I thought this would be a good opportunity to dispel some of the myths, and clarify some of the doctrines surrounding that. I have five bullet points here, and let me just go through those real quick. 1. I want to talk about *days* according to the Lord in the scriptures. 2. How long are the days of tribulation? 3. When will the days of tribulation begin? 4. What will happen during the days of tribulation? and 5. What is the purpose of the days of tribulation?

And so, I have a number of doctrinal bullet points, but so that this isn't such a dry podcast I just think it's important for you to shed your witness and the gifts that the Lord has blessed you with Julie, as you feel directed by the Spirit. Please interrupt me and chime in when you feel like you have something you want to say. Does that sound okay?

Julie: That sounds great. I'm good with that.

Eric: Okay. The scriptures talk about different types of days, like there's the *Day of the Gentiles*, the *Day of Tribulation*, or the *Great*

18

Millennial Day. Those are three of the days that I've studied. I think when we talk about the tribulations it's important to understand that just prior to the Days of Tribulation is the Day of the Gentiles. In my reading of the scriptures, especially 1st Nephi, 3rd Nephi, Doctrine and Covenants 45, and Isaiah- they make reference to the Day of the Gentiles, and I think it's important to understand this begins about the time of Christopher Columbus. Nephi talked about seeing 'many nations and kingdoms', and then shortly after that talked about a man who was enlightened by the spirit and navigated the waters, and found the promised land, so we know that when they talk about those great nations they're talking about Europe and a lot of the things that happened there.

The Day of the Gentiles, according to my understanding, is a day the Lord is taking a chance on Gentiles. Before this time, He always gave a chance to the house of Israel and His covenant people to see if they would become a holy people, a holy nation and throughout history those nations failed repeatedly. The Day of the Gentiles seems to be a day when the Lord is testing His people to see if they will turn to Him. This day has a distinct and definitive end, which end is when the tribulations hit.

Then we have the Day of Tribulation. There are so many scriptures that talk about the Day of Tribulation. When you read the scriptures just think about the phrases that you've heard: 'days of sorrow', 'desolation of abomination', 'great and terrible day of the Lord', the 'day of the Lord', the 'time of the heathen', the 'day of the Lord's anger'; anytime we read about the destruction of Babylon in a future sense, or the falling apart of the church of the devil, all these things refer to the Day of Tribulation. Because there are so many scriptures that go with this I won't read them, but I'll just post some notes on this podcast on Julie's blog if you're okay with that Julie.

Julie: Yes, I think that would be great.

Eric: Okay. And then after the tribulations we have the *Millennial Day.* There's just a little background on some of the main days of the Lord.

The second point I'd like to make is how long the Days of Tribulation are. This a little harder to understand or to put together through the scriptures, but I want to just go through that briefly. The days of tribulation seem to be seven years long. There's no reference to that number anywhere in scripture with regard to the Days of Tribulation, so you have to do a little reading and studying to find it.

The key verses are from Daniel: 12, 11, and 13; Revelation 11:2 and 3; and Revelation 12: 6 and 14. In those scriptures I just referenced, they each refer to a three-and-a-half-year time period; in other verses it's in weeks, and in others they give it in days, but when you do the math it ends up being three and a half years. Now, Doctrine and Covenants Section 29 and Matthew 24 both refer to those days. In Matthew 24: 15 and 21, the Savior put two different days together: The Day of Tribulation and the Abomination of Desolation which is two, three-and-a-half year periods. Add them together and you get seven years. That's just kind of a scriptural backing for how long the days of tribulation are, but Julie do you have anything you want to add to that?

Julie: I do. Thank you first of all for directing us to those scriptures. It's always really amazing to me as I hear you speak, Eric, or others speak as they ask questions or state scriptures, and for me the way it works is the veil will kind of open up and I'm shown scenes related to that specific topic that we're talking about; things that I've either been shown previously, or that I am currently being shown. As you were talking, the veil kind of opened for me, and I had visuals of several of the scenes that I see coming in the Days of Tribulation and Abomination of Desolation; some very tragic scenes, and some also glorious scenes as we have ministering angels and others with priesthood power from the other side of the veil that come to assist through those tribulations.

I have been pondering the last couple days about what the Lord would have us speak about today in regards to the tribulations and how bold I'm allowed to get. Anybody that's been listening to me for the last three years will notice that the message is getting more and more forthright, more bold, more direct and that we're giving out information in these podcasts that we haven't written about in the books. There are reasons for that as we get closer to the days that are soon upon us, we're going to see some very very difficult things. The message that I'm supposed to share is of one of light and hope, but also a voice of warning. And so I am trying to balance the voice of warning with helping to wake people up and not put them in a panic or a scare, and giving them hope and light and understanding that God has a plan for everybody is kind of a tricky deal.

We have a lot of people who are still not awake. They're still trying to wonder if what I see is going to really happen. A lot of people have great concerns about their friends and family members. Those that are believers, and those that are not. I find it interesting Eric, I've had three emails in the last week come in from listeners who are believers who have essentially tried to kindly let me know that I should not focus on the unbelievers, that they're not going to believe anyway, and that I should focus on the believers. I need to be very clear and in letting people know that I see it a bit differently than that. I do the best I can to spread the message as I hear it being told to me from the other side of the veil, and as the thoughts come and the visuals come to me, I am seeing on both sides the veil lots of non-believers become believers.

These messages that we do on these podcasts, while this may sound strange to some, I will be forthright in letting you know, these are messages for those on the other side of the veil as well, who are listening and hearing me and Eric speak as we record these, and then also as each of you who are listening to the podcast now play that, you have ancestors on the other side of the veil and watchers and observers from the other side of the veil who are not yet convinced that they need to join the Lord's fight on the other side of the veil.

So, while to some it may seem that we're not gaining forces of light being increased, I do get visuals and they will show me as the veil is parted, many many spirits on the other side of the veil that are going to the light even as we speak. As they realize that what we are saying is true, they can go to the light, that they don't need to be unclean before the Lord anymore, and that they can seek His face, and in so doing take upon them Christ's name and come to the light to help fight for the forces of good on either side of the veil.

My hope is that as we do these podcasts increasingly so, as we use boldness and people wherever they may be within the sound of my voice, will hear the conviction in my voice and in my heart, and in yours, Eric for you and for me together to be able to do some missionary work on either side of the veil.

This real, the days are upon us. I have clear memory, and I have clear conviction. I have been told yet again more of my mission just in the last 24 hours. And they have given me yet another witness in the last 24 hours of the importance of standing firm, standing true, and standing tall in the convictions that I have. I'm not going to go into detail as to how I have had this witness, but I will say that the Lord works in patterns with witnesses. I have had specific witnesses on both sides of the veil, letting me know that what we're doing is according to the Lord's plan.

I am grateful to those who are listening. I want to issue a word of caution to you if you have this playing around children right now. I feel it's important that you know that what we're going to discuss right now could instill fear in your children, and if I were going to be listening to this, I would listen to it with adults only. This not something I talk about with my children, and I have teenagers. I definitely would not be discussing this with young children. And I think it's important that you hear me when I say that. Now that's not because there's anything in there that some people consider- that's not child appropriate. I think everything that we talk about will be uplifting, if people can understand grasp the concept that the Lord has a plan for them. So listen to this first before you let your kids listen to it.

The topic of the tribulations themselves are very weighty. They're very difficult, and they come with some really hard things to discuss without causing fear to come into our hearts, and the only way we keep from having that fear and anxiety is by taking our concerns to the Lord, asking him if this message is true, and if what I speak about is true and accurate and will come to pass, which has been prophesied in the scriptures. I'm not going to tell you anything that's not already in the scriptures. I would just be putting it in layman's terms for how I see it in the views they've given me.

Having said that, if you are feeling fear right now, or if you feel fear during this podcast or after, recognize the source of the fear. I encourage you to go back and listen to the podcast that Eric and I did several weeks ago on casting out fear. It would be a good time to replay that podcast after you listen to this one. Eric, I don't know if that's even answered anything you said, but I just felt the need to kind of let people know that as we get into some of the nitty-gritties of this conversation.

Eric: That's great Julie. You know anything you want to say I trust is according to the spirit, so it's great. I really appreciate your witness about the other side of the veil. I love missionary work on both sides. I'm less acquainted with how it works on the other side, but to hear your witness as one who has gifts to be able to see those things, is really really cool to me, and it just seems to me things aren't always as they seem to us here on earth. It seems like there's always more going on than what we see.

Julie: There is. In fact, you know, if we could part the veil for people, and they could see how many different spheres and dimensions are all around us at any given time, I think it would be truly amazing for people to understand. I don't pretend to understand all of it by any means, but the glimpses that I get into eternity are fascinating to me. They're beyond my imagination, beyond the scope of what I can comprehend at this time. The more that I see, the more that I hear, and the more that I feel, the more of a conviction I have that God has a plan for us, and that we are not alone, and that we don't need to feel alone, and that we have so many people on the other side of the veil that love us, that are cheering us on, and they're rooting for us to help us as we complete our mortal missions here on earth. As we complete our mortal probation, as they have already completed theirs, or they will yet come to earth to complete theirs. I think it's just a beautiful plan that the Lord gives us families, and he gives us those who love us, to help us through this mortal probation.

Eric: Great, thanks for your witness on that, Julie. Let me go to bullet point number three then, with all that behind us. *When will the day of tribulation begin?* Now, while we don't have a date, or at least I don't, we do have some signs from the scriptures that we can watch for. And right there I just want to say, I don't think we need to be embarrassed if we're watching for signs. There's a little bit of a stigma I've noticed with *sign seekers*. Now that can have a bad connotation to people, but the fact is we're commanded to watch for the signs, and it happens scripturally in ancient times. People watched for signs in the heavens, and watched for things that prophets said to be fulfilled. So for those of you who are watching for the signs of Jesus Christ's second coming, don't be ashamed! Don't be embarrassed! And don't hold back! You can be vocal about this despite the persecution the world would give you.

When will the Day of Tribulation begin? Doctrine and Covenants 112: 24-26 is a good place to start on this one. It says, "And upon my house shall it begin, and from my house shall it go forth saith the Lord." 1st Peter in the New Testament is another one we can read to give us a clue about when tribulations begin. It says, "For the time has come that judgment must begin at the house of God. And if it first begin at us, what shall the end of them be there that obey not the Gospel of God? And if the righteous scarcely be saved, where shall the ungodly and the sinner appear?" Okay, so we learn from Peter there, that the time of judgment or the Days of Tribulation begins in the house of God.

Then lastly, Matthew chapter 24: 7 and 8: "for nation shall rise against nation and kingdom against kingdom, and there shall be famines and pestilences and earthquakes in diverse places. All these are the *beginning of sorrows*." So what we learn from the Savior there is to watch for the signs of wars among nations, famines, pestilences, and earthquakes in diverse places. When we see those things, then we know that the *beginning of sorrows* – and *sorrows* is another word for the Days of Tribulation. And that's all I have on when the tribulations begin. Julie do you have anything to add on when those days will begin?

Julie: Well, I've been told and shown that they they've already started as far as we've been in tribulation and the wars, the pestilence, and all these things have begun with the signs that are coming, and have come already, but the official start of the tribulations from what I'm being told by John and those on the other side of the veil that are helping in this mission to get the message out, is when that earthquake in the Wasatch happens. Now why that is, I'm not going to speculate. I'm just going on what I'm being told, what I'm seeing, and what I understand with the pits opening, with some of the middle-earth stuff and other things that I see that I'm not going to go into, and some of what I see going on in the world with dark government - actually every government is dark at this point - they've been infiltrated on every level and in every country.

With what I see the puppet masters doing - and there are some very, very evil forces at work that are planning this, and that are going to contribute to when this earthquake happens. There are a lot of reasons why you can have an earthquake, and as we know that there in the Midwest for instance, there are fracking institutions and companies that are causing or contributing to earthquakes. There are a lot of things that play into this earthquake and the Lord knows the times and the seasons of all these things, he's perfectly orchestrated these tribulations to begin at a time when the dark forces will come up and open as pits open.

As these entities and unclean spirits take hold upon the earth for a short time, they will essentially be allowed to rule and reign to a greater degree in the next seven years as the tribulations start- which I don't have an exact date on that either. I've been given some ideas, some times and some seasons, some things to look for, and sequences. I'm still waiting to see a few more of those in the coming months, and I could say that it wouldn't surprise me to have an earthquake this fall, but I've said that before and so you know it just lets you know we're getting closer.

If we had an earthquake this fall along the Wasatch, then I would say to you that that is the beginning of the tribulations and we could count seven years from this fall if there's an earthquake. Now it may be that we don't have an earthquake this fall and then you count seven years from that. The Lord doesn't always do this, but in cases of importance, he uses exact math. I would say that there are specific things that will fall into place as we look at the signs in the heavens with the Day of Judgement coming upon us.

Now we could take a look at some of the other podcasts we've done recently with the gathering of New Jerusalem, the priesthood, signs in the heavens, having been prompted to do those last three podcasts in the last week and a half or so; I would say that the Lord is definitely preparing His people for something very very huge, very very soon.

Now, I've caused a lot of unrest for some people because they are not happy with the boldness with which I declare some of these things; and I say to those individuals, what would you have me do? I am speaking boldly because I feel strongly about this message, because I'm being directed to do so, because we are in the final hours and the countdown has begun.

We are in the final countdown, of days prior to the tribulations beginning. How many days exactly? I don't know. But I know we had the solar eclipse last week; I know we have September 23rd with the planets aligning, and I know we have Yom Kippur, which is significant, and that we have the Day of Judgment coming after that. So we could have a matter of a couple weeks after the end of Yom Kippur, or we could end up going for another couple years. I doubt that's going to happen. My feeling is it's coming sooner rather than later because that's what they keep telling me.

But *soon* in the Lord's time is not necessarily *soon* in my time. I just know that we have a lot to get done, and a lot of people still to warn on both sides the veil- who are still not listening, still not repenting, still not paying attention, and that the signs around us are everywhere, and they have had family members and friends beg and plead with them to wake up, to pay attention, and they're being called crazy, or they're being neglected, or they're being ignored. We don't need to freak out about it because there's a plan for every single person the planet. But the plan that I've been given, that I agreed to, was that my voice would resonate throughout this world, and people would be reminded of the commitments they made to God before they came to this earth. I say that boldly, and I say that strongly; that it was given to me again today, that my voice will resonate with people; either for good or for ill.

I have been told I will be both loved and hated like Joseph Smith because I will have a message that will be that divisive for some individuals. That's not because it's a wrong message it's because it is a right message, and some people don't want to hear the truth. When we're talking about tribulations and everything that goes into the tribulations, I hope you can hear in my voice how passionately I feel about this. This war. This country's going to go to war; the tribulations are going to come, and if you sit on your bum and don't do anything about it, then we're accountable, and we have millions of people on this planet that are going to needlessly suffer.

The Lord does not want us to suffer just to suffer. He has a plan for every one of us. He gives us every opportunity to be able to repent and come to him before destruction comes. And he does not do this because he wants to injure us, he does this because he loves us, and he doesn't want us to have any more wickedness placed upon us to our utter condemnation. How about that, Eric? I can get on my tangent. If people don't know I'm serious after this podcast, I don't know what it's going to take. Really, you know?

Eric: Thanks, Julie. It's always a powerful witness to hear you talk about those things. I have one more thought concerning the timing of this, and when it starts, and so forth. In my spiritual ears right now I can hear lots of people saying, don't worry about when it starts, it doesn't matter and besides, "no man knoweth the hour", and that sort of thing. I just want to say that that response is a lack of doctrinal understanding of what that scripture means. When we say "no man knoweth the hour", we're not talking about when the tribulations start. That scripture is in reference to when the Savior comes and I just want to be clear, that is not what we're talking about in this podcast. What we're talking about, is the seven-year period prior to the Savior coming, and whatever time period lapses...

Julie: Sorry, let me interject here. No man knoweth the hour he comes specifically for his second coming; because there will be other visits- no man knoweth the hour of His second coming when he will come to rule and reign. Nobody knows that.

Eric: Right, right that's a good point. Because there are other visitations prior. No, that's a really good point.

Julie: Right.

Eric: And I used to assume when I studied the tribulations that - well I knew that they preceded Christ's second coming, so I thought to myself, "Okay well that's easy. As soon as The Tribulations are up, then there comes the Savior", but there is a time period between the end of The Days of Tribulation, and when the Savior comes, and *that* time period I haven't been able to figure out through scriptures or any other means.

Julie: Right.

Eric: Okay, so let's move on. Bullet point number four. This where it could get a little touchy. *What will happen during The Days of Tribulation?* I want to first start and really root us in the scriptures. Isaiah is one of the best to read, on what will happen during the days of tribulation. John the Revelator is another. I first want to point out, when I first started studying after reading Julie's books and other books, I wanted to understand what the tribulations really were. I was kind of astonished as I began studying Isaiah that Isaiah made six very specific references to the Days of Tribulation and specifically how many people will die during that time period. Now I know that's a gloomy topic and stuff but I think this so basic I think it's important for us to actually understand these scriptures, and I just want to go through all six.

Isaiah 1:9 – "the destruction before Christ's coming is likened to the days of Sodom and Gomorrah where only a few were spared." Okay so this kind of a metaphor a comparison that Isaiah wanted to make with the last days, he compared it to Sodom and Gomorrah.

In Isaiah 7:22, Isaiah used another metaphor. He was talking about how few animals will be left after the days of tribulation, but it will be enough to feed the few remaining people.

Isaiah chapter 10: 18 and 19: he uses the destruction of Assyria which was shortly to happen as a type and shadow of the destruction that would take place during the tribulations of the Latter Days. If you read in LDS scripture headings, it specifically says "few people will be left after the Lord comes again."

Isaiah chapter 13:12, Isaiah uses a metaphor of fine gold, okay, and as you know fine gold is very rare and he compares the rareness of gold to the rareness of man who will be found on the earth at that time.

Isaiah chapter 24:6 - This is the one where he's comparing the few remaining people on the earth to a forest, and how a forest is desolate.

Then Isaiah chapter 24: 13-14, he uses another metaphor. For those of you who are in agriculture, whether it's grapes or potatoes or whatever there's this concept of gleaning after you go through and harvest your field or your garden, where the tractor might leave a few potatoes along the side. This is the example that Isaiah chose to use as a metaphor for how few people will be left after the tribulations.

So, it's a bleak topic, but it's just important to understand what Isaiah and John the Revelator see is that a great majority, well not a majority, but a significant and substantial number of people will lose their lives.

Julie: Actually it is the majority. And again, not to be fearful, but that is the reality. I need to add my witness and testimony to what both Isaiah and John talk about, because I was shown the same things they were shown. They've made it very clear to me as John has been my guide and communicated - and even when I say that there are people that get all bent out of shape that I could claim that John the Revelator would be my guide. I speak the truth you guys. I'm not going to make any excuses, I'm not going to make any explanations other than to say I was shown the exact same thing that Nephi, Lehi, Lamoni, Isaiah, Daniel, and John were shown, and many many others in scriptures that have been both recorded here, and will later come forth in records that we do not yet have.

I'm not the only one that's seen this, there have been other people that have seen it, that are both prophets and those that were regular people in society that were shown these things. They are real, and it is absolutely true. Now what I've been weighing back and forth with Eric, and you know because I talked about this earlier, is how specific does the Lord want me to get with people to wake them up and say, listen, when we're talking about the fields being left the way they are with a few potatoes, I'm talking about the visions I have in my mind, and I hope people will hear me when I say I went for nine years keeping this to myself before I was given permission, and then commanded, to share my story.

Nine years of reminder dreams and visions, and memories of my near-death experience, and many close calls on the other side of the veil because of health issues and adversarial attacks. And I can witness and testify to you guys, I've seen this more times than I can tell you. They're horrific. And I'm not just talking about plagues or pestilence, or famines, or droughts. Those are scenarios, that are going to be horrific because people will be hungry, they will be starving, they will be crazy, they will be sick, and they will be dying in the streets.

But then there's a whole different level of the whole purpose of these Gadianton robbers; these puppet masters, and their evil designs of what they want to do. It will have both death and destruction from natural disasters, many of which are man-made, and we will also have other efforts made by the puppet masters to depopulate the world, specifically in the United States, because Satan, and Cain who reports to Satan, and everyone else who works for the puppet masters whether they know it or not who report to Cain, know that the end must come and their days are numbered. It's been prophesied. They've been on the earth this whole time too. They've been planning this for a very, very long time, and they are going to try with every effort that they can to destroy as much of the earth as they can, and to destroy as many people as they can, on both sides of the veil.

That is the endgame. If they can't get you to join the dark side, they will destroy you, and coming to the dark side is destruction, so either way that's the end game. Control, dominance, war, fear and destruction. With that, I'm talking about specific things of such wickedness that we can't even imagine because most of us would never dare think of such atrocities; worse than World War II, worse than World War One, worse than Vietnam, worse than any war that has ever been on this planet.

We will see atrocities on this planet and right here in United States. I don't want anybody to look me in the face in the future and say, "how come you didn't tell me. I had no idea they were going to try and do that." We know that there's human trafficking going on right now all over the planet. Most of us don't have any idea how horrific that is, but last week as I met with several individuals for GTRF, we're working with a few different companies, and some fundraisers that are going to help us with human trafficking. We're setting up rescue missions for human trafficking, for now, and going into the future and into the tribulations, because quite honestly, for the puppet masters, if they can't control you, they will eliminate you. That is their goal. And that means using you in any way that they see fit to make money, or to have dominance and power over you.

Now what this means to me is that last Thursday night and Friday night and Saturday night all night long, once again, I was shown millions of faces of women and mostly children who are being trafficked in this world, and especially in the United States right now. That's mostly what they were showing me, and they communicated very clearly to me that it will not be long before we will see that number grow exponentially. This is what we're looking at in the tribulations. If we do not go to places of safety, or we are not doing everything we can to be self-sufficient, and then rely on the Lord for all that we have with priesthood protection, we can basically count on giving up our rights to the Gadianton Robbers who would seek to destroy us. And that's where it gets really, really dark. Eric – your turn.

Eric: Okay. On that bright note...

Julie: Right?

Eric: I know this isn't pleasant to talk about, and Julie I know that you've seen a lot more than you've shared; specific details, gruesome details. I've heard Julie mention some of these things in passing. Sometimes she almost needs to vomit after talking about them. Julie is a mid-aged woman, mother from Kansas, and it's like, no woman in that demographic could come up with the scenes of horror that I've heard Julie describe. So, I know that you are not making this stuff up.

Julie: Thank you. I was 31 years old with an 8 1/2-month-old baby girl, and 3 year-old and five year-old boys. I was baking bread, I was making dinner, I was working for a jewelry company, I had a husband who was working as a medical malpractice insurance defense attorney at the time. We were living a very normal life according to American standards. My son just started kindergarten. I was looking forward to other than working on contracts for the jewelry company, being a stay-at-home mom. I used to make baby quilts, right? I did some of these traditional mom things that you do when you're in your 30s and 40s.

No longer. I don't have time for that, because this is such an important message. I woke up from that near-death experience a changed person. I knew that Father in Heaven loved me in a way that I could not even imagine, and I was shown things that were both beautiful and horrific from the beginning to the end of time. I was asking questions every day, and I still ask them every single day, multiple times a day: "why me Lord? What have I done to deserve this? Both for good and ill. Is this a blessing or a curse, because this feels like a curse to have these horrific images in my mind, that I can do nothing with. I can't breathe a living word to it to anybody."

And then they would school me, and they would come to my rescue when the adversary was beating me up like crazy, and having night terrors, and night sweats, and the worst nightmares you could imagine. And the reason I can talk about it the way I can talk about it is because I've had priesthood blessing after priesthood blessing, and I've had a lot of energy work done, and I've been able to work through the energy to be able to say, this my mission, this is what's going on, this is what's really going to happen, and I no longer suffer from the post-traumatic stress disorder I did. Anybody that saw what I saw, I guarantee you would suffer the same thing. There are no other explanations for why I have these images in my mind, and why I feel so compelled to share this message. No one does that who's normal.

Eric: (chuckles)

Julie: They don't do it! It's not a normal thing to do, right Eric?

Eric: You're right

Julie: You know I'm not normal. But by all accounts, my friends and family and neighbors that knew me never would have expected it. They still can't make sense of it, many of them. And I can't make sense of it, other than to say that I know this of the Lord, it's come from a supernatural being, it's come from an outside source, and I've seen the light and the dark to such a degree that I cannot have it stay within me without feeling like I'm going to just combust. It's so much a part of me, I feel so compelled, I feel so passionate about getting the word out, because if I do not, I am accountable.

There are millions of lives on the line if we do not each do our part to fulfill our mission, and every single person listening to this call knows I'm talking to them. It's starting to resonate with people that have been too scared and too passive, and I'm hoping that when you hear me this time, you're going to put that fear aside and you're going to cast Satan out of your life, and you're going to say to him, get thee hence, because the Lord is going to win this battle. The tribulation is going to be hard, but the Lord will win. The only way we can do it, is to wake up, get more light and knowledge, receive Christ into our lives, and then gather together as the family we once were, and that we are meant to become.

The gathering of the Lord's children is the next dispensation of time. We will go from the Gentiles in the fullness of times, to the Gentiles who have then become basically converted to Christ. We will go from the fullness of times to the gathering dispensation, and that is what we're getting ready to enter into. *The Gathering* dispensation.

Eric: Great, thank you, Julie. So on the last bullet point I have, *what is the purpose of The Days of Tribulation?*

I want to just start by saying that again, the Lord has always tried to prove his people collectively, not just as individuals. Since the beginning of time he tried to prove the faithfulness of nations. Early on, there was a lot of success. Through the city of Melchizedek and the city of Enoch, the Lord was able to prove those people, and they were translated. He tried to do the same thing with the Israelites after Moses became their leader. He tried to get the Israelites to also become a translated and righteous city that would serve him. They failed.

Many years later, in the early 1800s, he tried to restore the gospel to Joseph Smith. They had high hopes of becoming translated, very righteous cities who served God, again they failed. We read about this in Doctrine and Covenants. That day has been prolonged, and here we are at the "latter end of the latter days", as we've been told by Russell Nelson, that the Lord is trying again to see if we'll become that righteous people. It just seems like we aren't getting the message.

So what is the purpose of the days of tribulation? It's to see - well, let me go to Doctrine and Covenants section 112: 24-26. It says, "because there are those among his covenant people who have professed to know His name, and have blasphemed against Him, in the midst of His house." He's trying to test his covenant people who claim to know him, and go to his temple, but they blaspheme him in the midst of his house. So what is the purpose of the days of tribulation? In part, it is - I don't know how to say this eloquently - His covenant people are blaspheming His name, and He doesn't like that.

Julie: Well I need to add, Eric, something right here because it just keeps coming to me, and I'm not the only one who sees this, I'm not the only one who has felt it, I'm not the only one who knows this, but we need to wake up! We need to look around and take a look at our hearts, because many of us can recognize that we are living in the very days of the Pharisees and Sadducees.

Eric: Mmm Hmm.

Julie: That is where we are. If you look at the types and shadows in the scriptures, and you want to look to history from where we are, beginning into these tribulations, it is because we are living similar to the days of the Pharisees and Sadducees.

Eric: That's right. I agree with that statement. Another purpose of the days of tribulation is for our purification and sanctification. You can read about that theme in the scriptures. Anytime the Lord has a great work to do, he'll always try the faith of his people. And in the process of tribulation, they become sanctified and purified. They learn to trust in God more fully, and to rely less on the arm of flesh, and to simply just put all your trust in God, and realize that we can do nothing of ourselves. We need God, we need Jesus Christ in our lives to help us. And in that process we will become sanctified. Those who remain will be sanctified.

I feel like as I look around America, I've been frustrated naturally for years with the way we celebrate holidays. They have a tendency in my view, of being self-serving, and a little bit gluttonous at times. I know as I read the scriptures, the covenant people that the Lord wants are not a gluttonous, self-serving people. I feel like here in America we've been very blessed with resources. I've spent time in a third-world country, and only after I returned did I realize how good we have it in America, and I just don't know that we appreciate all the blessings that we have. And so, one of the other purposes of The Tribulations is to get us to turn to God, and to realize the blessings that he's put into our lives.

Julie: Thank you, Eric. I talked with somebody today that is having a hard time – worried that they're not going to be worthy of the Lord's protection and of His blessing when the tribulations begin. They have wayward children; their spouse is not fully awake, not even close. They're concerned that because of that, they're going to be punished because maybe they failed as a parent, or they're not doing everything they can to live worthy of the Lord's protection.

I need to make it very, very clear the message I got that I told this individual today – that is a false belief, and that's a false tradition. The tribulations will come and upon his housetops he will cleanse his church first, and there is truth to that, but just because we suffer and we go through hard things does not mean we went through and did anything bad, and it's not because we are undeserving or unworthy of his protection. He protects us in ways we can't even imagine.

There's warfare going on all the time, and just imagine what would happen if there wasn't that protection, how much more we would suffer? He only lets us suffer according to our individual plan that was designed with him in the pre-existence before we came, that we agreed upon, to allow ourselves to suffer to become like him, and in many cases, join the fellowship of the suffering. So just because you're suffering now, or you will suffer later does not mean that you weren't worthy, or that you did something wrong, or that somebody doesn't like you in heaven. The opposite is often true.

The Lord does punish those who rebel against him, but he does so out of natural consequences in most cases. When he allows us to suffer, he allows us to become more like him, and I think we need to recognize the tribulations for that purpose. It will give us a higher purpose in why we have our suffering, it's given me purpose in my suffering, and I can tell you guys right now, they've made it very clear to me I didn't have a near-death experience and get sick, and I don't have all these health problems because I sinned. I am a sinner, I'm a very imperfect person, and the only way I have any shot at ever returning to Father in Heaven is because of the atonement; but that is not why I had a near-death experience, and it's not why I'm sick, and it's not why I suffer now. It's not because I did anything wrong. I think some people really need to hear that. That's a false tradition that's been passed down.

Eric: Thanks for that witness, Julie. I have one final point here. And when I read Doctrine and Covenants section 88, the more I read and study that section of scripture, the more I understand the whole winding up scene here as the Day of the Gentiles comes to a close.

Here's the simple bottom line of the tribulations: Jesus Christ is going to come and reign on this earth, and to do so, this earth can't exist in its current Telestial state. It needs to be Terrestrialized; it needs to receive more glory; there needs to be a group of people here who are righteous and worthy to accept him and pave the way for him. We simply are not in that world right now. We have to create that world, and again, Doctrine and Covenants section 88 talks about the increase of light with each kingdom of glory. If you think through that a little bit, you'll realize that there are a great number of wicked individuals, with wickedness and atrocities taking place on the earth, and those simply can't exist when Christ returns. I think of it as a geographer or science-minded person, it's just the way physics has to take place that we need more light on this or earth, as we turn into the Terrestrial Kingdom.

Julie: I like that. I love the science behind it. I look at it like energy, with vibration going from one level of vibration to a different level of vibration. As we go to a higher vibration and operate at that level, the lower vibration cannot exist, and the converse of that is true as well. In order for us to raise the vibration of the earth, and therefore have the earth essentially be translated into a millennial state, we have to have resurrected and translated beings who carry it forth into that state, and that means raising the vibration of the individual on the planet, and in the earth, and everything on the earth. And it is science. It really is just abiding by eternal laws. God doesn't make those laws; he just uses the laws to fulfill creation.

So you know, he is an infinite and eternal God, the atonement is real, it can heal all things. Anything that passes to the other side – plants, animals, vegetation of any sort, an individual of any kind of creation – go on to a different sphere. It's not the end, so those that pass to the other side while tragic and difficult for us to endure, it will be a blessing to those who go to the other side. They basically graduated from their mortal probation and they get to go on to another probation wherever they may be in the eternities, and that's not something that we need to be sad about, although maybe how it comes about is going to cause us a lot of grief.

Eric: Thanks for that recap, Julie. You said that so much better than I could have. So, really glad you chimed in there.

Julie: Oh, I don't know about that. Eric, I appreciate everything you said, is there anything else you feel like we need to cover today?

Eric: No, I think we've covered it. Let me just testify and give you the last word Julie. I like to think of The Tribulations as Goliath to David. If we boldly face our giant tribulations of the last days, I know that we like David and his giant will overpower them, in the name of the God of Israel, under the power of his promises to Abraham, Isaac and Jacob.

I know that we can overcome The Days of Tribulation if we acknowledge that it lies on our doorstep, and if we arm ourselves with righteousness and the power of God as mentioned in 1 Nephi 14. And that's my witness.

Julie: Thank you, Eric. I appreciate all that you've shared. I appreciate all the scriptures that you've given us.

You know, my mind keeps going through some of the things that I wish I could say to you guys, but I don't want to motivate you out of fear. I want you to be motivated because you can hear the truth coming from our voices, and you can feel the spirit resonating in your soul and in your heart to motivate you to do good works.

The truth of the matter is, that we're looking at a country that will soon be invaded. We already have sleeper cells of lots of different countries here on our soil, waiting for their cue. I don't want to be one of those individuals that watches my husband get shot, or my children get eaten, or somebody next to me get raped. Now that's graphic. It's gross, and it's awful, but that's the reality of what we're looking at, and I hope that you will do all in your power to get answers from the Lord, to take these messages to the Lord, whether it's this message on the podcast, or any other. Ask the Lord if this a true message, if I'm a true messenger, if what I speak of is true. And then do with it what He tells you to do, and you will be finding safety and rest in his atonement, and his Gospel. Not in my words, or the words of anyone else. You will find rest in your soul, and peace in your soul to put the anxieties and fears aside, because God will give you that peace and comfort to your heart.

I witness and testify to you that these are true words that I speak, that I do not lie, but I share it out of the goodness of my heart because I love you, and I want you to be as prepared as possible to either meet your maker on this side of the veil, or the other side of the veil, whatever and whenever that may be. We need to do all we can to help our brothers and sisters because that's what we covenanted to do before we came to earth, and that's what we've covenanted to do, those of us that have taken upon us the name of Christ. And I leave that message with you in His name. And I hope and wish you the best as you go throughout your endeavors in the coming weeks. God bless you.

TRIBULATIONS 102

EPISODE 33

Julie: Welcome to the Julie Rowe Show. Today is Tuesday, September 5, 2017. Eric and I have another great show in store for you today and I hope that you find it insightful and informative. Eric, I'd like to welcome you to the show and turn the time over to you.

Eric: Thanks Julie. In our last episode we talked about The Tribulations. The intent there was to lay a doctrinal foundation for The Tribulations; what they are, what to expect in those, some ideas about when they would start, and the purpose of those tribulations. It was very structured, but today I thought it would be good to just loosen up a little bit and go a little bit more according to the spirit and whatever the spirit would like you to say about the tribulations Julie, and I'll do my best to ask questions as directed as well.

Julie: Okay

Eric: Why don't we go ahead? Has anything come to your mind since we last spoke about tribulations?

Julie: Absolutely. My heart's been rather heavy with several things on my mind. Most recently with everything going on in Houston as those who are listening can imagine, I know I'm not alone in this. It's heavy for several different reasons. First and foremost, because of the devastation down there and the number of people that are being affected with Houston being such a large city. And secondly because we have hurricane Irma about to hit the Florida coast and it's hitting Puerto Rico and several of the islands out in the Atlantic before it will hit the United States, or off the coastline.

Quite honestly Eric I'm fired up. I'm really fighting emotions that are, I guess you could say triggering emotions. I know that the Lord's plan to allow people their agency. That's an eternal principle, the law of agency. I know God has a higher plan for entering into the tribulations and I know I've said this many, many times. But the human side of me is frustrated with the wickedness that I see on this planet and that I see coming to the planet still.

I'm not sure how many people are aware of what's really going on in Houston and I what I mean by that is we know that the media lies to us. We know that we're not getting the full news. We're not even getting a portion of the true news. We're getting lied to about everything and that includes what's going on or what happened in the Houston area before this hurricane Harvey hit land. And now we've got Irma coming, and I have been waiting essentially for my cue to talk about this hurricane and this incoming hurricane Irma. The reason I say that is because we could have done a podcast a couple weeks ago on hurricane Harvey and I talked to Eric about it and I just didn't feel like it was the right time yet to expose some of what I feel is happening out in Houston. So we're not going to spend an entire episode on this but I do want to touch on this because this is a type and shadow for what I see has happened many times before and will yet happen again, as we go through the tribulations.

When we're talking about the dark forces literally stirring the pot. And symbolically speaking, but literally and figuratively when we look at hurricanes and the technology that is being used that was developed several years ago, and China, Russia, and the United States all have the technology. Several years ago the United States worked with various scientists and they developed technology and have been working on technology that affects the atmosphere, the ionosphere, and basically weather changes and patterns.

We've had Al Gore and others bumping their chests for years now about climate change and climate control and it's a bunch of lies. They are creating a great deal of the climate change and it's all about manipulating, controlling, depopulating, and then taking hold so that they can put their dark forces to work at a greater capacity. Now this might sound strange to some people who are uneducated about what the governments have been doing throughout these countries. The puppet masters are fully orchestrating things like HAARP, that claims to have been dismantled, but hasn't been. There have been universities involved in this that have helped participate on a scientific level.

The government has utilized our tax money for research on climate control and manipulation. They're continuing to do it, including things like chemtrails, which some people think is hogwash. I'm here to tell you the chemtrails are real, and that's minor compared to some of the crap they're doing. You know, in this documentary that we're doing, we're going to expose some more of it. This documentary is not just about Julie Rowe and her life it will follow the biography basically, but I'm going to basically expose some other things that have been going on in the world, specifically in the United States, and we're going to put this in the documentary. They're going to back it up with research and other connections that are going into the documentary so that they can take what I have to say and have other voices that have expertise in some of these areas so that I don't just look like the crazy lady coming out with conspiracy theories.

I'm here to tell you guys a lot of these conspiracy theories are true, and if you're not familiar with it it's time to get familiar, because the atrocities that have occurred in Houston and will yet occur makes my blood boil. I try to keep it in check because I know that the Lord is in charge and that the adversary wants me to get upset and angry, but I hope to use these emotions that I'm feeling to propel us forward for good and to convince others and to testify and warn and witness to other people that we have got to stand up and take a stand for righteousness and be aware and awake about what is going on in our environment.

This world is absolutely being destroyed by the dark forces and it will come a point in time where there will be so much dark energy on the planet we will be left with nothing but the choice to rise to a higher vibration so surely would be destroyed utterly. The Lord will transition this world from dark energy to light energy but it doesn't just happen coincidentally. Irma also, being a category-5, that does not just happen you guys. Nor does an earthquake that's a 10. There are reasons for it and there's actual technology that can contribute, if not cause, but usually contribute to already weak areas in certain locations.

Officially the tribulations start with that earthquake that's in the Wasatch. I continue to ask the Lord if I've seen and am hearing that correctly and I'm still being told that's when the portals open, that's when the pits open, that is when it officially starts according to the Book of Revelation with time being kept with the three-and-a-half years and the other three-and-a-half years to make seven. Prior to that we'll have earthquakes in diverse places and we're going to have fires. We see a lot of fires going on around – don't even get me started on some of these fires that are in Montana and Washington and Idaho, destroying beautiful, beautiful countryside. There are so many things going on that often feel like they're out of our control, right?

So what do we do when there's chaos going on around us and we see the wrong but we don't feel like we have the power to correct it? Well, I think first and foremost is educating ourselves and our loved ones that there are wrongs being committed so that we can be educated to know what we can do that is in our control.

My heart goes out to those who are in Houston and surrounding areas those that are in Florida and in the islands of Puerto Rico Cuba the Caribbean and other places out there that are being hit right now and will soon be hit this weekend. I feel literal heartache with that and I know that there are many, many people being affected by these things and ultimately what is the purpose for why these puppet masters would want to create such catastrophe?

Well, there's money in war at least for those who are causing it. This has been the case from the beginning and that's the case now. Power, control, and money. Some say you can do anything or buy anything with money and I say that that's a bunch of hogwash. The one thing you can't buy is peace of mind and a place in the kingdom of God. The individuals who are masterminding this seek not to do his will but seek to do the will of the devil. And you know I just I don't have words for it Eric, because it's hard for us to imagine that someone could be so satanic, so carnally minded, and so devilish that they would seek to hurt one individual, let alone millions of individuals, and to do it purposely.

I'm here to tell you guys unfortunately that is the case and then they're using lower-level people that don't understand to carry out their wrongful actions. I want to mention one important factor and I want you to open your minds to why this would be. If you look at all the major wars in the last several years that we've had and ask at least in part of what it's about, it's about oil. Then you look at the location of where they've chosen to put the hurricanes and I think it speaks volumes when you've got a city like Houston.

They've done it with Katrina, they did it with Sandy, now they're doing it with Irma and they're affecting gas prices and they're doing it on purpose and one of the reasons is so that they can claim there's a gas shortage again, which is a bunch of hogwash as well. So they can they can increase gas prices, they can increase oil, they can increase fuel prices and then they can claim there's a shortage. This will affect every American and in the short term that's their plan.

They can help "crash" the economy. It's one more factor and then they can claim that they have food shortages and other things like food rotting on docks because they don't have oil or the fuel to be able to get the food transported where it needs to be in the stores. It's all lies - you guys have got to see the writing on the wall that this is where we're headed. We have not seen anything. Gas prices will continue to increase.

At the point in time the troops come in I've seen gas prices exponentially high. Very, very high. I'm not the only one who's written of this, and with that comes mass starvation. People are not able to get to work, they're not able to get to their job, they're not able to get to schools, the places they need, and they're not able to get to the grocery store. Then they don't stock the shelves because they haven't transported them on trucks or on trains. This a domino effect and we're seeing the beginning of what I was told the hurricane is before the earthquake. A week ago Friday before hurricane Harvey hit, I was told – I guess it was two weeks ago. I was told by the spirit as I saw this in vision and then saw the Wasatch Wakeup, that these hurricanes are the hurricanes before the earthquake, the earthquake being the Wasatch Wakeup. And then I had two other people, one person texted me, and two other people emailed me saying that they had had revelation regarding these earthquakes as well, and these hurricanes asking me if I'd been told anything about that. With that I want to turn the time over to Eric and have you share an experience you had, if you can Eric.

Eric: Yeah that sounds good. This would be one of the first times I've ever shared any of my revelation publicly. But on June 26, 2015 - this was in the middle of a duration of receiving lots of dreams, and I would always record those dreams - but on that day I had a two-part dream and I recorded it like this: "there was a man who stood before me as if he was standing on a beach. He formed a three-dimensional map on the sand beneath him and the map was of Houston. And suddenly the map or the three-dimensional city of Houston sunk into the sand then it was covered by water and then my dream ended.

And then the second part kicked in and I was at my parents' place in Southeast Idaho and it was shaking violently, so I knew we were in an earthquake. I didn't have any understanding of what that dream was and I have to say that I have absolutely zero connection to the city of Houston. I've never been there and have never thought about it. And so that was always weird to me. Now I always tried to understand why would I have something shown to me concerning

Houston? Also concerning the second part of the dream, I've never been in an earthquake and have never experienced the sensation of it, but in that second part of my dream it was shaking violently and so it was just really peculiar and odd for me to have that dream.

As Harvey has been unfolding I thought "I wonder if that's the dream I had with it being covered in water" and then of course now I'm wondering if my dream was giving any sort of insight as far as sequences of events I would naturally believe that one of the next things we'll see is some shaking somewhere.

Julie: I appreciate that Eric. Taking note that there have been some earthquakes out in northern Utah and southern Idaho in the Soda Springs area that have reached a few hours in several directions from there. They've had a 5-5.3 they're currently having earthquakes right now as we speak and all of that area is connected out there to the Wasatch. They are now projecting a possibility of a six or seven out there at any point in time.

You know I did see earthquakes out in the Rexburg and Idaho Falls area. We're going to see those. I don't talk much about them because the Spirit keeps guiding me to wake up the Wasatch and because that has such a pivotal role in the tribulations, but we will see more earthquakes out there in Idaho as well. It's amazing to me, that when I was given that instruction or that understanding a couple weeks ago about what I was seeing in Houston, and then Florida coming as I prayed to Lord about that and I was told - that was before Irma was even on the radar and I asked the Lord "am I hearing that correctly, hurricanes, with an 's'", and I didn't have clarity at first; I thought maybe it was because there was going to be another hurricane that came right into Houston or somewhere in the Gulf. Then they panned over to Florida and out to the Caribbean.

I have come to understand - how do I say this - just because I see it doesn't mean I can say it, and sometimes when I see it I don't always understand it. More so in the last six months I've been hearing from the other side. I will get a visual and I will hear something in regard to that visual, but very often now for whatever reason, I'm being told things more than I'm actually seeing them and I'm not sure if that's just because the devastation coming is going to be so horrific that they're protecting my heart. I've seen many of the scenes before for several years but as we get closer it triggers me emotionally and I think tender loving Father in Heaven is protecting me from having to see so much of this devastation as we see it unfold in real time.

The other message I've been given as I've asked why I'm seeing less now it seems, than what I was prior, is that they want me to work on my hearing skills, and this is something I encourage everyone to do. We have ministering angels on the other side of the veil, we have our ancestors who are ministering to us that love us very much, and even if you don't have a gift of seeing you are all entitled to have the light of Christ and many of us have the Holy Ghost, and through our ancestors they can give us warnings and can help us out. This seems to be happening to me more and more, I feel like I'm being guided by the spirit through thoughts, words, deeds, and feelings in my heart. I can't express to you guys enough the emotion in my heart.

I've said it before and I'll say it again, I don't know when this earthquake is, but it's close enough that I'm being triggered on an emotional level and I'm seeing things that they showed me 10 years ago and they're bringing them to my mind again now, and so having said that we're going to talk a little bit more about some of the scenarios that I see as we go into the tribulations and try to help some of you understand a little bit better about what we might be in for.

I see mass exodus of people on foot travelling to escape from floodwaters from all kinds of storms; winter storms that have them trapped in locations until snow melts, and then mudslides. I see in certain areas rivers overflowing but because of drought the water just flushes away. I see droughts and famines. I see children orphaned in the street. I see human trafficking at levels that have been unprecedented on this planet; I see women and children and families being torn apart. I see families in hopes of finding food and safety and refuge aligning themselves with the dark forces; some being completely deceived, and others doing it willingly, similar to that in the days of World War II.

So Eric, you know we visited a little bit about some of what I want to share today. I said it several times that we're living in the days similar to what the people were experiencing on a smaller degree of pre-Nazi Germany and there's a lot that goes into this, so I'm not going into those details, but, Americans do not know their history. They have not been taught it, and that which they have been taught has been false history, revisionist history, everything from why we had a first Civil War and why we're going to have another one.

The first civil war was not just about slavery, and there was a lot more that went into that. The Founding Fathers were inspired. The document that went into the Constitution and the Bill of Rights and everything that this country was founded on, as far as the Founding Fathers, were of the Lord's orchestration and they were designed for higher purposes. It didn't take long for imperfect men and women to distort the truth and to trample on the very document that the Lord brought to pass.

I'm going to read from a book because this is a first-hand account from a man named Walter Rohloff, and he sent me this book that I've been reading *Under the Wings of the Almighty'*. I'm just going to read part of it because I think coming in first person from someone who's lived through World War II will be more impactful for those listening than to hear it for me. I lived in Germany and I learned this history from living over there in ways that those who've never been to Germany will never be able to understand. Just like I can't imagine what it's like to live through world war when I haven't been through one.

Note: Julie then reads several pages from the book, *Under the Wings of the Almighty,* by Walter Rohloff, of first hand experiences of life under the Nazi regime.

All right I know that was a lot of reading but I felt like it was better to read it so you guys could hear it first hand from an individual who lived through it. We're headed for World War III and we're looking at similar things coming so how do we combat that?

So this is where my heart goes out you guys because I see the types and shadows. I lived in Germany for three years from 1986 to 1989. I went to Berlin before the Berlin Wall came down in the fall of 1989. I've been in a communist country. I know what happens when people are having food rations. I know what happens when they don't have cars to drive; when they have to wear uniforms to work and school, and they have very few freedoms. When the mark rate was so high they could hardly afford to put food on the table. It was like the Lord gave me just a small glimpse of what was coming to America back when I was 16 years old.

I do not have words to express in my heart the emotions that come up when I see what's going on in Houston and what will be going on in other areas the country. What's already gone on and is going on. I see that they mess with EBT cards and the other ways people get their food stamps and their other benefits. What happens when we have individuals who are not able to get toilet paper, food, baby formula, and the other necessities of life for their children? It does not take long before we have angry crowds and we will see rioting in the streets. We're going to see it here with the aftermath of Hurricane Harvey. We're going to see it with other hurricanes and earthquakes and other natural disasters but we're also seeing it because they're man-made creations for them to start both a civil war and a world war.

It is their goal to start civil war in the United States, which was prophesied by Joseph Smith that would start in a small city of Chicago which would one day be a large city. Today there are millions of people in Chicago, and we're going to see riots in the streets and it won't be long. We're going to see other riots throughout the country like what happened out in the Carolinas and those areas, they're bringing in the rioters; they're paid rioters being put on the same buses as these fake KKK guys on the same buses of the black lives matter. It's absolutely absurd but because we have corrupt media bought and sold and owned by the puppet masters we are not getting true news. We're not getting truth. And we have too many people who've been infiltrated in every institution of government and every single church that are there and willing to cover up and work for the dark forces and we've got to put a stop to it.

I am not beyond believing that we can't stand up and make a change for history just because things have been prophesied of does not mean that we have to sit by idly and let them do it. We are warriors. That's what I signed up to be and that's what those who are listening to this podcast need to be reminded of. We did not pre mortally agree to come to the earth and let Satan rule and reign and do whatever he wants. We signed up to come and to live and give the good fight which is to stand up for truth and righteousness and to stand up for the plan and that plan includes helping every single one of God's children come to light in whatever form and fashion.

To me that means I'm going to do everything in my power to warn my neighbor. I hope you will do the same. You may not talk about crazy conspiracy theories that Julie Rowe is talking about on this podcast and how the government's able to control weather, but I hope that you will at least mention that God has a plan that when you see someone in need or when you see someone standing on a street corner with a sign saying they're hungry that you won't pass them by.

You may not be living in Houston or Florida or anywhere else where there's going to be a natural catastrophe anytime soon, but I promise you it will come to your doorstep if not sooner than later. You will be in that position and we know that when we provide for other people the Lord provides for us. I witness and testify of this, that we need to be very careful about who we pass by on the street because we may be that very person begging for food in a very short time.

I hope that those that are listening will know that no matter what is said, no matter what is done against me or anyone who decides to stand up for truth and righteousness and to spread the word and to spread truth wherever we may be; I hope that if you're listening within the sound of my voice you will take courage from the

Lord; you will know that he has a plan for you, and you will know that as you have courage in standing up for truth it doesn't matter if we're on this side of the veil of the other side of the veil, we can find rest and we can find peace.

That is the only thing you guys that gives me any kind of comfort and peace right now is the word of God and his promises he's made to me and every one of his children; that there's an atonement, that it's real, that there's a plan of Salvation, that we have everything being orchestrated just according to the Lord's plan, that he's allowing these things to happen, because if he wasn't, he could come and in and one fell swoop, take care of the entire dark side in an instant.

But that's not the way our God works. He created this earth for us; he created this earth so we could become like him, and in that he's allowing us to participate in spiritual warfare and soon we will have physical warfare on the American continent but with that we will have angels of light coming to help us and coming to our rescue. We will have translated, resurrected, and angelic beings who will come with priesthood power that will blow them away.

I witness and testify to this that no matter how dark it seems the light side is winning. They're winning now and in the eternities, and they will always win because that's how it goes. You cannot win when you fight for the dark. I witness and testify of this, encouraging any and all who are willing and able to go to the light. As I bring you truth and I bring you understanding because God has all power. And I say that in his name. Amen.

Julie and
the LDS Church

Episode 34

Julie: Hi, welcome to the Julie Rowe Show. Today is Thursday, September 7, 2017. I've got Eric on the line, just wanted to turn the time over to you Eric and welcome you to the show.

Eric: Thanks Julie, and thanks to everybody for tuning in. We've had a lot of feedback from people on these podcasts, and we're just delighted that you are responding so well to them. It's humbling to us to hear that they're having a positive impact in your personal lives and in your relationships, and your witness of things to come, and your witness and understanding of the plan of salvation in these latter-days. And we're grateful for your positive and uplifting comments.

In some of those comments, messages and email and so forth, we've had some questions come in from time to time, and there have been other doctrinal topics and so forth, that we've just talked about doing, but didn't quite know how to fit them into a podcast. With all this coming together, we think we can put an episode together on some various topics, especially related to The Church of Jesus Christ of Latter-Day Saints and Julie's involvement in the church, and then add a few other questions. Also, in the spirit of lightening things up, some of our podcast topics have been a little heavy recently so this would be a good way to lighten things up. So, Julie, if you're okay with it, I have a series of questions for you. Is this going to work?

Julie: Sure.

Eric: I want to start with your interactions in the church that you are a member of - The Church of Jesus Christ of Latter-Day Saints, and I want to ask you about your attendance in church and temple activities.

Julie: What would you like know Eric? (laughs)

Eric: Well, I mean, this may feel a little bit like a Bishops interview. I think this is just an opportunity for you to just to answer a lot of these questions so they stop popping up, you know.

Julie: Right, yeah. Because I keep getting these emails from people because there's all these rumors going around about my church membership and activity and there are just a lot, and I can't dispel all the rumors, that's not the goal of this. But, if we can put some of it at bay, I think that's good. I just don't have time to respond to all the emails that are coming in, and I don't want people to think I'm ignoring them, so I think we might as well just go ahead and address it.

I am an active member of the LDS Church. Now, according to LDS record, to be considered active you only have to go to church once a month. I am much more active than that, I actually go every week unless I have health issues. So, if there's someone in my home ward that doesn't see me, I'm either traveling and attending another ward when I go to a different location, or I'm home sick with some of the health issues that I deal with, so I try to go to my meetings every week.

I'm assigned a visiting teaching route. I go to the temple as often as possible. I used to go about once a week, sometimes twice a week, with all my travels and now being about an hour and a half away from the temple, I'm lucky to be able to go about once a month. Although, it's been more frequent than that, depending on what's going on with my kids' sports schedules and stuff like that. It's kind of hard, because I have to be able to leave early enough in the morning to go do a session, like maybe an 11:00 session in order to get back to pick my kids up from school at 3:15 pm. So, that's my biggest thing is just being a little bit further from the temple right now, but I'd say I go to at least once a month and sometimes twice a month.

Eric: That sounds like about another million members or two that I can think of (chuckles).

Julie: Yeah, if I had my way I'd probably go there every day because I love going to the temple. So that's about how often I can go do a session, sometimes I can go more frequently than that because I can go do initiatories or sealings, and I can get in and out in a half hour to 45 minutes instead of needing to block out 3 hours.

In fact, not that I need to share this with people, but maybe I shouldn't announce, I'm going to the temple on a date night with my husband coming up here pretty soon. We have a date scheduled on September 15th and we're going to go to the Kansas City temple and then clean the temple afterward. I also help clean the temple for those that are familiar with that. I enjoy doing that, there's a different kind of experience you have when you clean the temple.

Eric: So, do you and your family members have callings in the church?

Julie: Yes, actually. My husband was teaching youth Sunday School a couple months ago and was recently called as a counselor in the bishopric in our ward. I have been a teacher in Relief Society, I don't know for how many months, since last fall, they called me as a teacher in Relief Society, so that's what I do right now.

Eric: What is it like being someone, you know, I guess in the public spotlight as a member of the church, does it create trouble for you at all?

Julie: It has, but not anything I can't handle, depending on what ward I've been in. I wrote my first two books in Arizona in 2014, where we lived for 15 months. Prior to that, we lived in Overland Park, Kansas for 11 years, or just under, then we moved to Arizona in 2013. In 2014 when I wrote those first two books, we only lived there a year and a half, so members of the ward didn't know me at all when I moved in. Most of them had no idea I was writing books, I was very low-key about it and I had a handful of friends that knew that I was doing that.

Then, by the time the second book came out, we moved because my husband got a job in Iowa, so then we lived in Iowa for 22 months; he actually stayed working in Iowa, the Spirit told us to move to Kansas last summer, so we moved the 1st of July of 2016 to Kansas and we moved an hour south of where we used to live. So, we're in a different stake, but we're in sister stakes and members of our stake used to be part of the same stake years ago, back when my husband grew up, so we know a lot of people in the stake, although I've been really low-key out here.

We bought 20 acres on a property out just south of Ottawa Kansas, and we did that for several reasons. According to my husband, he doesn't quite know why we did it, other than the Spirit told him to do it. My understanding is, I saw this house and property in vision, and it's going to be a weigh station for people coming through from the east as some of the tribulations start, so we'll be here as a weigh station for a time before we go west.

And it's nice to live out in the country, energetically for me it's very therapeutic, it's very calming. I work from home with the relief organization and then doing energy sessions, so it's nice to be able to, like today, sat out on my front porch and just made phone calls and I did three sessions with clients, and so it's very relaxing out here. It takes about 15 minutes to get into town. We have a town of 10,000 people and that's about 45 minutes north for us to get up to Olathe where we have metropolitan Kansas City.

Eric: So, Julie, speaking of property do you or your husband or GTRF have any other properties?

Julie: We do not personally own any houses. GTRF actually does not own any properties. The way that we're structuring it is, individuals reach out to me and ask if they can provide a safe house and they are privately owned by the individuals and then we work with them to develop the safe house properties to get them ready for people coming through and to work as refugee locations. So, GTRF does not own properties at least not right now, and I don't know if we will, and I only own the house that I live in.

We have owned, in all of our marriage, five houses and two of those were rentals when we lived in our house in Overland Park. And then, we had our first house when my husband first got out of law school when we were in Wichita Kansas. So, they've always been private residences and our current house is a private residence. We purchased it off of my husband's income, so any of the income I've made from the books, or any income that's come in for GTRF, none of that's come to me personally for this property. Everything we're doing so far on this property has come out of my husband's income, and that's how we qualified for the house and everything. I know there's some rumors going around out there, wondering what I'm doing with the money that I've made.

So I've put all of my book money, with the exception of a few thousand dollars, and paying off the credit cards that we had from moving from Arizona to Iowa when we got some credit card debt. I paid that credit card off with some of my book royalties, and then the rest of it I've used for travel to go around and speak and to buy books to give away for free, or to basically get the message out. I've just put it all back in and same with the GTRF funds, anything that's come in we've used that for supplies or for travel to be able to connect for funding and other things, so, I keep all of the business expenses separate from personal finances, so my taxes are clean.

Eric: Gotcha. Okay, I want to steer us back to the topic of the church and some more things there. Do you sustain The First Presidency of the Church and the Quorum of the Twelve Apostles?

Julie: Absolutely. Yes, I do. I am so grateful for what they do, they have amazing abilities and gifts and they have an incredible stewardship. I can't imagine the pressure they must feel as prophets and apostles and disciples of Lord Jesus Christ, and of his servants on earth, to represent The Church of Jesus Christ of Latter-day Saints. I'm grateful for the work that they do. I have absolutely no doubt that they've been called of God and that they are servants of God as true messengers. I'm forever grateful for the living prophets we have now and for those that have lived on the earth before. It's interesting, I hear these people that say things like, "Joseph Smith was a true prophet," and I always want to say, "What do you mean was? He is!" (laughs)

Eric: Yeah.

Julie: I see him on the other side of the veil, right, and he's still working. Same with Moses and Elijah and Noah, like they're all still working on the other side of the veil as prophets and in the capacity of leading legions of spirits over there. So anyway, and I see the same thing pretty soon with President Monson, when it's time for him to pass through the other side of the veil, he'll go on, and he'll complete the rest of his ministry on the other side of the veil, as he leads and guides and directs those and teaches those on the other side of the veil once he passes.

Eric: That's nice, thank you for that witness. I want to ask you another question. With regard to some of your gifts. Now, I've demonstrated scripturally and doctrinally on previous podcasts that all of God's children are able to receive the gift of prophecy. You are obviously a very gifted person in that area of being able to see things, past, present and future. And this gets sticky for some people who think that you're outside of your bounds of seeing and saying what's going to happen in the future and stuff. So, I want to ask if you claim to receive inspiration, revelation or direction in behalf of other people?

Julie: No, not at all, I never have. That's a consistent message that I will continue to give. I do see things about people and I am told things about people as it pertains to my mission and my stewardship with what I understand I've been called to do, but, I have never shared that with people, I don't tell people that even when I see it. What the Lord has told me is, Julie just because you see it, doesn't mean you say it. So, for instance if I see something that pertains to one of my siblings, I don't share it because I don't want to take their agency away and the reason the Lord shows it to me, is so that I can understand it or I can be empathetic or I can help support them in the way that I need to support them.

The same goes for anybody else in my life. Most of what I see pertaining to other people, if I can discern things that they're struggling with, or health issues, or other things, when I can see into their energy or whatever, there are specific guidelines the Lord has on both sides of the veil with respecting people's agency. And that's where stewardship comes in, in part. I'm continually being taught by the Spirit, that we can receive revelation as it pertains to ourselves and those in our stewardship, like our children and those if we have a church calling or something like that. I have been given certain insight if you will, because of my eternal mission that has been made known to me that I was set apart on the other side of the veil.

Later on, say we fast forward 10 years, it'll be very clear to people at that point, or most people, why I was given the gifts that I have and why I can see what I can or what I claim to see, and they'll understand that there was a bigger mission involved here than what most people recognize right now. And so that's why I can boldly claim what I do and I can stand up for what I say I see, because it's important for them to understand the difference between different types of stewardship. I don't hold any keys, I don't hold any priesthood authority and I don't claim so, and there's a big difference between somebody who has keys and authority and priesthood keys and authority, or stewardship over church calling versus being called by the Spirit as a covenant people to stand for Christ and stand up as a witness for Him.

And then even later on, I know that I will be given certain callings or keys to important aspects of the gospel that come later. I'm not talking priesthood authority in the way that we're looking at right now, I don't want people to be confused, but, I've seen that I will be set apart for a calling later on, and that's what I mean by that. That doesn't happen until well into the future after things have deteriorated and we're in the tribulations. There's a big difference between having personal revelation and having revelation for the church or for a body of people, and I've never claimed that, and I still don't claim that.

I see things in the world and on the other side of the veil and in my own life, and in the United States, because it specifically pertains to my mission. And they continue on the other side of the veil to tell me, that the reason I need to see this is because it pertains to my mission specifically, and to my life. With that, they let me know what I need to know, when I need to know it, and how I need to know it, so that I can advance in my understandings in light and knowledge, so that I can be who I need to be, whenever I'm supposed to be that, and I'm still trying to figure that out. I ask every day, multiple times a day, why are you showing this to me, or why am I hearing this, or what am I supposed to do with this, and it's something we need to all ask ourselves when we're given any kind of revelation. We need to make sure that the revelation is coming from the right source, right, because Satan can give us all kinds of false stuff.

Eric: Right. It sounds like you receive revelation that may be pertinent to other people, but it's not your role to tell them what to do with that, or you basically respect people's agency and you don't tell people what to do, based on your revelations.

Julie: I am passionate about agency, that's what this premortal war was about, that's what the war is still about, is agency, it's one of the many things that we fought for and that we're still fighting for on both sides of the veil. It is absolutely critical for the plan that we have agency. I would never assume or want to take anyone's agency away, that is contrary to my nature; it's contrary to the Lord's plan. I want only to support His plan, which is first and foremost to know that there's agency, and that we have an eternal atonement that's been offered to us.

And so I am constantly weighing what I know with what I'm allowed to say, because in giving the knowledge that I have, if somebody listens to a podcast or hears me speak somewhere else, or meets me and we have a discussion, or they read the books, or however they come across whatever knowledge I might share with them, they are then accountable once they hear that knowledge and once their spirit resonates with that, and only the Lord knows what they know and what they understand, then they become accountable.

It's not something to be taken lightly because if someone's not ready to hear something and they reject it, then it's to their condemnation not to their salvation and exaltation. Only the Lord knows when someone has actually heard a message, or when it's actually resonated with their spirit to the point that they have an understanding and knowledge to act which is why we can't judge either, right? I mean, I have an understanding about some things about probations that I've lived and premortal memories that I have, and things pertaining to my pre-mortal experiences, as well as my life here on earth, that some people just don't have for various reasons.

So, just like I would hope people wouldn't judge me for claiming that I know that, I don't judge them for not knowing it. If it's not part of their plan and it's not their not time to know it, the Lord's not going to give it to them. I'm a hundred percent comfortable with people either accepting or rejecting this message if they're not ready to accept whatever truth, because I believe that God has a perfect plan for every individual, and we only advance in that knowledge and that light as we're ready for it, as we accept it for ourselves with agency. If I were to try to force anything on anyone, it's contrary to God's plan, it's contrary to agency, and I'd be working for the devil and that's not who I work for.

Eric: Great, great, well said, Julie. I'm a witness that everything you said is true about your nature. I've known you long enough and well enough to know that you respect agency. Do you claim the authority to proclaim doctrines, new doctrines, unusual doctrines on behalf of the church?

Julie: Well, I appreciate that question; I know you asked it earlier. I don't claim any authority. I have no authority, and not only do I not claim authority, I don't have new doctrines to present. There has been nothing I've said that could be construed or misconstrued (even though people are doing it) to say that I have publicly ever said to somebody that there's a certain doctrine.

     Now, there might be a new way that people have never thought of that doctrine, because their eyes are opening, because of the verbiage that I use, but I, myself, have never proclaimed doctrine nor do I plan to be the one to tell people what certain doctrines are. I don't think it's my role, I don't find that as part of my mission. I might be there one day to testify and warn of certain things that come forth later, through proper keys and authority of the church, but I myself do not have the role, as far as I understand, at least nobody is telling me that will be the person that's going to announce any of that stuff. And if there are people on the planet right now, and there are some, and I won't name names, but there are some that are claiming authority and are dissenting from the church, and that are claiming that they have certain authorities to be able to change or transition people away; those individuals are leading to apostasy right now, and they take part in the great apostasy I see coming.

Eric: Interesting. Speaking of apostasy and that kind of thing, are there any doctrines in the church that you are unsatisfied with or you think that are incorrect, that you think should be changed or altered?

Julie: No, that's never even crossed my mind. I see a lot of cultural things that really get on my nerves. Quite honestly, there are a lot of things, and I see it exponentially growing in the church, with false belief systems and cultural things that absolutely irritate me, but from a doctrinal standpoint, there's not a single doctrine I take issue with. In fact, if anything, I want to witness and testify of the importance of the doctrines, because they go hand-in-hand with the ordinances, which are necessary for us to take part in to advance in our powers, priesthoods, and understandings.

So if there's someone that takes issue with the doctrine, my word of caution to them is what has been told us by our living prophets and apostles, which is, doubt your doubts before you doubt your faith. I have a sure knowledge of these doctrines. Not only do I not doubt them, I have a sure knowledge of them and the importance they play in our lives.

Now, there are cultural things that have become like doctrine to some people, but that doesn't mean they're doctrine. There are cultural things that have infiltrated the church and Christendom in general, that are false beliefs and false traditions that have been passed down, that I believe need to be broken before we can progress into the Church of the Firstborn. That is not my place to go around and try to correct everybody's behavior. I have actively worked at trying to get rid of my own false beliefs, and you can do that through praying to the Lord and asking him to show you what your false traditions are as is witnessed in the scriptures as types and shadows that we know upon the heads of the third and fourth generation, is the condemnation to the traditions of their fathers. Those traditions can be good and they can be bad, and we have a lot of traditions now going four generations or more into the church that have been passed down that need to be broken.

Eric: Okay. In the last three years of your message being more public, have you ever been approached by church leaders for a disciplinary action of any kind?

Julie: No. I've had conversations with every bishop and stake president, because I've gone to them and I've given them my books, and I've told them about the work that I'm involved in. I had a stake president in Arizona that didn't know anything about me, and he got a call from one of the members of the Seventies, that was concerned when I was going around speaking. He was concerned that I was selling books in the Mesa inter-stake building. Other than that, the church didn't want to lose their tax-exempt status, and so even though the individual who scheduled us at the inter-stake building, which is a public building - they use it for book signings and all that kind of stuff all the time - their only concern was they didn't want me selling books on that property from a tax exempt standpoint. That's the only time I've been called into a stake president's office.

I had a couple interviews with my stake president in Iowa; I first went to him and gave him my book. And of course, he was trying to make sense of, like many members of church, how can she be getting this revelation and doing these things, but she doesn't have "authority?" And then, we had some conversations, so I could explain to him what I was involved in, because I was brand new to Iowa, and all he heard was the rumors and stuff that were going down. Once he met me and we talked, he was nothing but gracious. I have never even come close to having any kind of church disciplinary action. In fact, I've got three of my previous bishops that are members of GTRF now.

Eric: (chuckles)

Julie: It's amazing to me, the things that people say. But, I can understand the concerns people have, because they've got these ideas in their mind, which again go with tradition, and they've never come across somebody like me as a member of the church, and so it gets them out of their comfort zone, they don't know how to put it in the box of where I fit in. You know, how does she fit in with what we understand with the traditions of their fathers.

Eric: And the easy assumption is that she's doing something a little different, therefore she's apostatizing and she's going to lose her membership status before too long.

Julie: Right. Well and when my books came out, they came out a year after the whole Kate Kelly incident, where her movement was being really aggressive, with you know, trying to protest about women getting the priesthood and stuff like that. So she had just been excommunicated, same with some other people, and so there has been heightened sensitivity to people like that, who by all appearances start out looking like lambs and in the end they're attacking the sheep and are not who they pretend to be.

Or, in some cases, I look at somebody like Kate Kelly, and my heart goes out to her, because I think originally it was probably well-intentioned, and she is listening to the wrong voices. And, so I was compared to Kate Kelly by several people, and there are still people comparing me to her. I don't want to speak ill of her or anyone else, I just think we're all on our own journey, our own path. I don't agree with anything she does, I am probably her polar opposite when it comes to some of the views that she has, if somebody were to actually know my heart.

But, I do know that we will see a day when things in the church are going to shift, and we're going to go from having the way things are structured now to being far different when the Lord takes the reins. That's because we will transition into a higher vibration and a higher way of living things, so we won't need some of the programs and stuff that we have in the church.

Eric: Thank you for that.

Julie: At least not to the same degree, you know we've got a lot of programs right now because it's what people need on a Telestial level.

Eric: Yeah, that's right. I'm a witness to that doctrine, by the way. I have another question or two concerning the church. Have you in the last three to five years had any correspondence with members of say, The Quorum of the Twelve, Seventy or even The First Presidency?

Julie: Yeah, well I'm glad I can finally speak about this. I've had dozens and dozens of people email me and ask, and people come up to me when I've spoken in public and ask me, "does the prophet know what you're doing?" and all that. My understanding from the Spirit is that they actually have someone assigned to monitor my website and to monitor the work that I'm doing. I see that in vision. They've even shown me who it is that's doing that, and they keep an eye on me, just to make sure that I'm not saying anything inappropriate that's going to make them uncomfortable. I don't have proof of that; it's only what I've been shown by the Spirit, so take it for what it's worth. I'm not claiming any factual information there; I'm just telling you what I understand from the Spirit.

The only conversations I've had have been through an email that I initiated in the end of December 2015, to the first part of January 2016. I was shown in vision for about three months, a lot of people were calling church headquarters starting in 2014 when my books came out; a lot of concerns about who this Julie Rowe was, and I came out of nowhere right, so all of a sudden this lady shows up and she's claiming revelation and they had concerns. So, they called Elder Ballard's office, Elder Eyring's office and Elder Oaks and some of the others. For whatever reason, I don't know why if maybe Elder Ballard is over certain things, the Spirit told me that a lot of people were calling Elder Ballard more than some of the other apostles. I don't know if that's true again, because I'm only going on what the Spirit's told me, but that's what I understood.

So, at one point I was instructed by the Spirit to call and just have a brief conversation with Elder Ballard's secretary, which I initiated just as a friendly call to say hi and thank you and I'm really sorry, this is Julie Rowe, and I'm really sorry for all the people harassing you. And that was it, and that was the purpose for my call and it didn't go anywhere, and it wasn't supposed to.

Then I called on another occasion as directed by the Spirit, to call Elder Eyring's office and talk to his secretary, and to let her know that I wanted to get a message to Elder Eyring that I have started a relief effort, my nonprofit organization, and to let him know about my third book coming out, because I knew at that point that they knew about *A Greater Tomorrow* and *The Time is Now*, and we had just had the lunar eclipse a few months before and all that negative press. I just wanted the church to know that I was doing the relief organization that I had set up, and I didn't want them to hear about it from somebody else; I wanted them to hear about it from me and just give them a heads up when media stuff happened again.

I saw in vision in 2014, that once this earthquake happens, there is going to be a media circus surrounding my name again. Because I didn't know exactly when that would be, and I didn't know when the earthquake would be, or when some of this documentary and other things would come, I just didn't want the church to be caught off guard. It's a real nightmare for the church on a PR side, to have loose cannons out there and I wanted to minimize that for the church, because I have great respect for the Brethren and for everything they're doing.

So, I was prompted by the Spirit to call Elder Eyring's office, his secretary said she suggested to me that I send Elder Eyring an email. So, that's what I did. I constructed an email and send it to Elder Eyring at the end of December or first couple days in January. Within two weeks of sending that email, I got a reply letter in the mail. I found it interesting, I was instructed by the Spirit to sign my name as Julie Rowe on the email and to put my - I didn't put my membership number or any of that right, I didn't put my mailing address which at the time was a P.O. Box because I was living in Iowa. I was unlisted in Iowa, and except for church leadership, no one in Iowa could see where I lived because of death threats and other things.

The Spirit instructed me when we moved to Iowa, to just put my mailing address for leadership to see so nobody can look me up. And so I knew that the only way that they could mail a letter to me was if they knew exactly who I was, or they looked it up and they got my membership records and mailed it to my P.O. Box. I did that purposely, because I was shown in vision that I was going to get a letter back. I was told what the letter would say roughly, and about how long it was. I saw that in vision a week before it came in the mail, and that's exactly what happened.

Now the reply I got back was from the Secretary of the First Presidency, in behalf of The First Presidency, thanking me for the kind email and letting me know that they do not comment on the writings of others and they wish me well in my endeavors. And that was the basic gist of the letter and I've had no communications since.

Eric: Hmmm, interesting. Thank you for sharing that.

Julie: Sure.

Eric: One final topic with regard to the church. Actually let me ask this question last of all, and then I'll move on. Because of your gifts and so forth, do you call yourself a prophetess or a seer, or do you claim this title for yourself?

Julie: I don't call myself anything, Eric (laughs).

Eric: (laughs) There are probably plenty of other people doing it for you.

Julie: I go by Jules, j-u-l-e-s, j-u-l-e-s, j-u-l-z, or Julie. A couple of my friends call me *Queen* every now and then (laughs), because I get very uncomfortable with that.

Eric: (laughs)

Julie: I don't call myself anything and I don't claim any of that. I have other people that have tried to give me titles, like you know, trying to say I'm a seer and stuff, but, I have spiritual gifts the Lord's given me and I have no titles and I don't really want titles, I don't really like titles.

Eric: Ok, fair enough. Now, I want to shift gears, still in relation to the church, but I want to move into the future. For those who have read the book Visions of Glory, Spencer in there talks about a large earthquake taking place in Salt Lake and then shortly following there was a meeting in the conference center in Salt Lake, I believe, or it might have been the tabernacle; it was a solemn occasion and there were a number of coffins at the front of the building and those coffins held the bodies of members of Church leadership. Now this is kind of a sensitive issue, but I just wanted to see if you have similar insights to what Spencer shared in his book there.

Julie: Well, I haven't actually read that. I've had a lot of people ask me if I've read 'Spencer's' book and if I've met him. I have met him and I've had conversations with him. I was given his book by two different people that were close friends of mine that were the only two people at the time that knew of my story, and neither one of them knew each other and they both bought me the book. I read the first third of the book and it resonated very much with my story, it was almost verbatim what I'd been shown. And then the Spirit said, okay don't read anymore. And so I put the book down and then two months later my second friend gave me the book and the Spirit said okay go ahead and start reading again.

So I did a quick read through, but honestly it was like a skim read because at that point, I was writing my own books and I was traveling so much and doing things and the Spirit basically said, no that was in '13, so it was right when I was having visions about my books coming, and the Spirit basically said, okay it's important for you to know who this person is and that his books are kind of preparing the way for your books, and he has his mission but don't really read it because you need to keep your story, and not get it convoluted with his. So I don't remember that part of what you're talking about, so I'm sorry I don't really know but I can only say what I know, which is that I have seen that about half a dozen of the Quorum of the Twelve will pass to the other side in the next several years.

Eric: Would you go as far as to link that event to some sort of future event following thereafter, like say the Church of the Firstborn?

Julie: I see most of those individuals passing before the Church of the Firstborn comes. So like, I see six of those brethren passing to the other side of the veil due to old age, mostly. And then some younger Apostles will be called to fill their shoes the best they can; nobody fills the shoes, but you know I mean, to take that office.

Eric: Hmmm.

Julie: I do see some similar things taking place in Church leadership to what Joseph Smith went through with Oliver Cowdery and Sidney Rigdon, and I see a little bit of that going on, but for the most part those apostles that we lose, we lose them because they pass to the other side of the veil due to old age. If they go from another way, I haven't been shown that, so I just know that I've been told and I see that at least six of them go to the other side.

Eric: That's interesting. I've always been interested in a quote by Joseph Smith who said in effect, "if you stay with the majority of the Quorum of the Twelve Apostles, you'll be on the right side." So that, I just wonder if Joseph had any insight of that event and he was giving us some prophetic advice, you know.

Julie: Right, types and shadows for our day as well we know that in the scriptures. And I was taught the importance of working in councils a long time ago and the importance of working and staying with the majority of the Brethren as well. There's a reason that those brethren work in councils as a majority, and I learned in college the importance of how they work together as a unified council and there's power in that unification.

I see in the Church of the Firstborn; it being set up in councils similar to the patterns in the heavens. For those that are familiar with the patterns of the heavens, you have a council, you have a presidency of three, you have your 12, and that presidency with the twelve makes it 15, and then expands out to 24, and the council goes to 48 then 72 and on out to 144. That's councils of men and women with separate councils, working together in a unified form. So, that's what I see with the Church of the Firstborn.

And with my relief organization, I've been instructed to have a board of directors and the board of directors is part of the council that I have. I have been instructed to pattern it after the way it's patterned in the heavens and to work through councils so I don't make any decisions on my own. I don't take that authority upon myself, whether we're talking about spending money on certain things, or where we decide to agree to have certain safe houses or any other endeavor that we have. I guess you could say as the president of the company, I have final approval, but I seek my counsels.

I have a first and second counselor essentially that work in a presidency with me, and then I have a women's council and I have a men's council, and they work together over certain aspects of areas and there's areas of specialty that we have. There is real power in those councils, because all of those individuals bring their gifts to the table and then it takes a lot of pressure off me, but also I'm just one person, I can't come up with all the inspiration that we need, and I'm not supposed to. So, it's really nice to have those council members.

Right now, I have established a council of 24 men. And then, I've got about half a dozen of the initial twelve put together, and in the next month or so I should have the rest of the women's council which is what we call our ACE team. Our ACE team is the number one team and they oversee things like hygiene kits, education, healing, kind of more of the traditional what the LDS Church knows about like, Relief Society type stuff. Then we have the *A-team*, which is over the men, who are area specialists and they help us with what we're going to do with the rescue mission, especially in the human trafficking side and being able to prepare things that we need for that like overseeing any kind of transportation needs and stuff like that, that we have for rescuing. I don't know if that answered it, but you got a really long answer for whatever it is (laughs).

Eric: (laughs) It's great. You covered everything. So I feel like we've had a pretty good array of questions. This should answer a lot of people's questions on this topic, and I hope it's been uplifting and beneficial to those who are listening, it has been to me.

I'll just close with my testimony, that The Church of Jesus Christ of Latter-day Saints is God's kingdom upon the earth. I know that it's led by inspired men and women. I know that we have the priesthood and saving ordinances and the fullness of the doctrines that pertain to our salvation, and I'm grateful for those. And so I'm grateful for my membership in the church.

Julie: Thank You Eric. I appreciate your testimony of that. I too want to add my testimony to leave no doubt in the ears of my listeners, wherever you may be, that I know that Joseph Smith is a true prophet as is every prophet that has lived on this earth, as representatives of the Lord's gospel, and that we have a living prophet, Thomas S. Monson, who is the leader of this church in modern times, and that we will soon have another living prophet, as the time comes for President Monson to pass to the other side of the veil, that we will have our living prophet then come that has been called upon and fore-ordained by the Lord. I know this to be true.

I have a testimony and a witness that I give to you, that the Lord works through small and simple means and that through these men and those that work with him, in the counsels in heaven as well as on the earth, the Lord brings to pass His righteous purposes.

I testify and witness to you that we have an organization that is on the earth right now, that is exactly what it's supposed to be and exactly where it's supposed to be, doing what it's supposed to be doing; that the Lord loves his children; he is directing The Church of Jesus Christ of Latter-Day Saints, and he's directing many of his children all over this planet preparing them for the next level of their growth, insight, knowledge and understanding. I have no doubt of this.

I know that the keys and ordinances of the gospel have been restored as we have them thus far, and that the Lord is orchestrating exactly according to the plan he had fore-ordained before we ever came to this earth and before it was ever designed. I leave this witness and testimony with you, knowing that as we do all we can to stick to the basis of the church and to the ordinances of the gospel as we fulfill our divine rights and our obligations and our duties that we covenanted to do, we can be able to progress eternally into the heavens as was designed and orchestrated and is being put forth by a loving Father in Heaven who wants us to come home. As we do this, we can gather home on both sides the veil; we can bring the family home to safety and find rest in His soul. And I leave this testimony with you, in the name of Jesus Christ. Amen.

MISSIONARIES CALLED HOME

Julie Rowe: Welcome to the Julie Rowe Show. Today is Tuesday, September 12, 2017. I've got Eric Smith on the line and we're getting ready to do another great podcast for you today. Hope you enjoy the show. Eric, welcome.

Eric Smith: Thanks, Julie. This one may be a little more off-the-cuff, so, I don't know where it's going to go, Julie, but I have a couple quotes and thoughts, and we've talked about these subjects for a while, so I'm just going to start with a little historical background and then, as usual just add your insights and any comments that come to your mind.

Julie: Okay.

Eric: I've been thinking about missionary work, right, and I want to read a little quote by Joseph Smith that goes way back in the early days of the church. One of the first things he said—I believe it was that meeting in 1830 when they organized the church and there were Saints all in that little room, right? And he says, "It is only a little handful of priesthood you see here tonight, but this church will grow until it will fill North and South America. It will fill the world." That's from the conference report of April 1898. I've thought about this a lot and, you know, we aren't there. While the Church of Jesus Christ of Latter-day Saints has had good steady growth over the years, there hasn't really been anything explosive to the point where we could say that the church has filled the world.

Now, fast forward. In 1998, I was working at a scout camp in Southeast Idaho, and there was a stake president who was just called as a stake president. He was from Pocatello, and we were talking and he told me that he was set apart by Elder Boyd K. Packer. In this blessing by Elder Boyd K. Packer, he was told that his "children would live to see the day when *hundreds of millions* would join the church." I always thought that was really interesting. This man was the same age as my father, so, that meant to me that my generation would live to see that day when hundreds of millions would join the church.

So here it is 20-something years later and, while we've seen some strides and progress in the church growth, we aren't to that point where Joseph said it would fill the world. Now as we study last day doctrines, and having talked a lot about transitioning from the Telestial church to a Terrestrial church, I believe that that day is soon at hand when the church changes gears. So, I'm left with this question of how we are going to fill the world with souls who are members of Christ's church, and fulfill both Joseph Smith's promise and Elder Packer's promise to the stake president. Do you have any thoughts on that, Julie?

Julie: I think that's excellent; great points to bring up. The first thing that comes to my mind is that we are in the dispensation of the gathering of the Lord's elect, and that in this dispensation we have been charged with bringing more of the children of the Lord to the church of Christ. What I see there is a transition where we have those that are of the house of Ephraim, and then others who are members of the Lost Tribes that come back, and joining forces together, bring about great and eternal works of righteousness through the gathering from the four corners of the earth, mainly through the 144,000, which will go out to preach to all the world and set up cities of light throughout all continents.

I think it's a beautiful picture that the Lord gives me to be able to see, to feel, and to hear some of the great things that are going on, on the other side of the veil and some of the great things that are going to happen on this side of the veil in the coming days. There really are no words to express to those that are listening that which I have in my heart when I think about the high and mighty things, the things of a greater day coming, which is why I was given the title of *A Greater Tomorrow* entitling the first book that was written in 2014.

It really is the time, the time is now for us to prepare and to be gathering in preparing for the great gathering; the great gathering being first and foremost, that's which takes place in the last days prior to the second coming of our Savior Jesus Christ, the great gathering being initially starting from several walks of life throughout all the different continents, but eventually leading into the next dispensation, as we go from the gathering of the Lord's elect, the dispensation that will be in the seventh dispensation as discussed in the prior podcast.

I encourage you to listen to that podcast if you haven't yet on the Davidic servant and the presidency with the Davidic King. It all goes hand in hand with the mission that the Lord sees in gathering the Lord's elect.

I witness and testify to you that these are eternal truths which we'll have and will be brought back to the earth as we go into the Millennium. Preparatory to that millennial state, we must have the gathering on both sides of the veil. I see this as an intergalactic gathering that goes on with the entire family. What do you think about that Eric?

Eric: Well, Julie you're talking about this greater tomorrow and this great gathering and those are exciting things to think about. I still see those as off in the horizon, off in the future a little bit.

Julie: Uh huh.

Eric: Now, there are those who are thinking right now, "But wait. We have been gathering for a long time, we have been gathering from the four quarters of the earth." And, you know, we have missionaries in all countries and all parts of the world. And we are bringing people into the gospel, and yet we still don't see that moment that Joseph prophesied of, you know, filling the earth, so there's a bridge to cross here and it's this bridge that I'm interested in. There are a few things that need to happen before that great day. One of those things, as I see it, is the Day of Tribulation.

Julie: Right. And Joseph Smith is still working on the other side of the veil leading people over there as essentially, a master general of a great army in the dispensation of the fullness of times with the stewardship he has. I yet again see him coming to the earth to fulfill his rightful place and preparing for the Messiah to return. Joseph Smith with the visions he was given and the doctrines he was given and brought the restoration to the planet, has a mission still yet unfulfilled here as he has been sent to the other side of the veil, but will return to help in the great gathering. I see him doing that on the other side of the veil, and I see him doing that on this side of the veil. So his prophecy will come to pass.

I see millions of people, hundreds of millions of people, joining the church of Christ, those from all walks of life. If you can imagine thousands of people coming from the Lost Tribes who have a portion of the gospel, some having a fullness and others that have very little, coming together with those who have, as the remnant of the Church of Jesus Christ of Latter-day Saints, gathering together at Adam Ondi-Ahman in a great meeting where the keys of the priesthood will be restored to the Messiah.

Eric: Awesome! I really get excited when you talk about Joseph Smith coming back to the world. What a blessing it's going to be to meet him one day.

Julie: Right. He's a beautiful man. He has a great mission still yet to fulfill in correspondence with the gathering.

Eric: That's awesome. So as I was mentioning this bridge that we need to cross, before getting there, we still have dark days ahead in

The Tribulations. One of the events that you've discussed that takes place at the beginning of those tribulations is a *call home.*

So imagine we have 60,000 plus missionaries out in the world right now, and you've had a whole bunch of people email you about this, mostly mothers who have sons and daughters out on missions, and they've been so curious to see what's going to happen with their children. Some are anticipating the tribulations so near that their children are actually hesitating to put their papers in right now, and it's just a big concern to know what to do with these missionaries.

Julie: Right. Well, it is a concern, and I can relate firsthand. My son just got his mission call and he is supposed to report to the Provo Mission Training Center on October 25th. I've been shown very little regarding his mission. For a long time, they weren't showing me anything and now they're showing me a little bit. I'm not going to tell people publicly where he's been assigned to go. I want him to have a chance to go out as a missionary and not as Julie Rowe's son, and also just for protection for him and those who would seek harm if they knew where he was going. Also, because I can give clues and things here and there about the timing of things as I see them, but everybody knows that a timeline gets a little bit tricky and if I were to give too much information, I kind of give myself away on some things because if he's getting his mission call and reports the MTC on October 25th - at least that's his assigned date to report, and then it's a two-year mission in the LDS Church -if I were to say too much, then people would have a better idea about some of the timing of the tribulation. I do anticipate that missionaries will be called home early, that several already actually have been for various reasons.

It seems like an alarmingly increasing rate, there have been missionaries being sent home for accidents or for medical reasons. I don't know if it's just because I'm at that age where my son has friends, and I have friends that all have missionaries out so I hear more about them now than I did when I was in my 30s, but I'm hearing about a lot of missionaries that are coming home for random reasons. I feel in a small way that the Lord has already started gathering his missionary's home as we transition from a church that has been in the United States sending lots of missionaries overseas to foreign countries.

There are fewer and fewer missionary calls going out abroad and many, many missionaries in the United States are being sent to different places in the United States rather than going foreign. Although we are still sending missionaries foreign, statistically speaking I believe that the number has gone down which is one of the signs that I was given would happen as we get closer to the Tribulations starting, and those that are in other countries are being sent out to serve in their own countries across the world.

Additionally speaking, I see that we'll transition from having the missionary program that we do right now, and having that be essentially revamped so the missionaries could, for a time, be called to special missions preparing gathering places in their own cities and in their own towns and in their own states or locations throughout the world, still being able to do missionary work on a global scale because of social media and other things that we have going on.

I've had confirmation of this and I've had personal witness of this and I want to bear my testimony that as these transitions happen, as these changes happen, it will be for our good; missionary work will continue through the Tribulations. In fact, we will see an increase in missionary work during the Tribulations, not less missionary work.

Eric: Interesting. I want to support this idea that you've mentioned about the missionaries being called home. I like to look to doctrine and quotes from scriptures and other General Authorities in the past and I have five good ones. I think they're worth reading and I want to start with Doctrine and Covenants 88:84. This portion of D&C 88 is talking a lot about the last days and the calamities that will fall. It says:

> *"Therefore, tarry ye, and labor diligently, that you may be perfected in your ministry to go forth among the Gentiles for the last time, as many as the mouth of the*

Lord shall name, to bind up the law and seal up the testimony, and to prepare the saints for the hour of judgment which is to come."

When I hear this, *bind up the law*, it reminds me in this portion of D&C 88 that it's talking about the laws and glory and light and knowledge and doctrines that exist in various kingdoms of Heavenly Father's universe and in the plan of salvation. When you *bind up the law*, to me, signifies you've reached the maximum capacity that your current kingdom is able to endure for a time. So "bind up the law," in a sense means, "You're done. It's time for"—right guys? We've been at this preaching for 180 plus years. The Lord is ultimately going to say, "you're done. It's time for me to do my preaching." And that's the beginning of the Days of Tribulation.

Julie: That's correct. I appreciate you talking about that. When I see "bind up the law" on an energetic level, it is literal. I see the school of the prophets in my mind. I see future schools of the prophets, if you will, and I see in these classrooms on the other side of the veil. And then those on this side of the veil, as the time that's been given, and I see an actual binding of the laws within a book; the law of the prophets, or of the kingdoms, in the order in which it was established in the heavens. I see an actual binding.

The Lord is bound to do His part when we do ours. When we've done all that we can do, then he then fulfills all of his promises to his children. It is after we have preached to those who have the word, even of the Lord's children, those that are a covenant people, after two warnings have gone out, it is then time for the Gentiles to have the word and everyone else is given the word.

There has been talk, and people have taken notice about my two books following that pattern, and I witness and testify that as my job as a witness, or as the witness, you can see that there's a pattern there that has taken place. In the first book of *A Greater Tomorrow*, the second, *The Time Is Now*, and the third one, which will go to all the nations, *From Tragedy to Destiny*, and I witness and testify of this truth and of this pattern that was established in the heavens, given to me by directive from the Lord through John the Beloved.

Eric: Interesting. I like this idea of three warnings kind of being a complete set of warning.

Julie: Right. It's all been patterned with the estates, but also, it's all been patterned with probations as well as offices of the priesthood being deacon, teacher, and priest.

Eric: Yeah, yeah. Very interesting. There's another quote by Ezra Taft Benson, a former prophet of the LDS Church, and he also spoke of this future event when missionaries are called home. Let me read this. "The time of the Gentiles refers to that period of time extending from when the gospel was restored to the world, to when the gospel will again be preached to the Jews, after the Gentiles have rejected it. The rejection of the testimony of the servants of God by the nations of the world will bring the consequences of greater calamities."

Julie: Right.

Eric: Here's another one. Brigham Young in Journal of Discourses Vol 18 says, "When the testimony of the elders ceases to be given and the Lord says to them, 'Come home. I will now preach my own sermons to the nations of the earth,' all you now know can scarcely be called a preface to the sermon that will be preached with fire." And he goes on talking about fire, earthquakes, tornadoes, and so on. So again, that's the Tribulations. So it's saying your missionaries will be called home before the Tribulations.

Julie: Right. Now, there's a two-fold layered purpose in that language bringing to attention—and this will make some people nervous that I say it, but I speak truth and my job is to witness to you so that later on if things don't manifest the way you've conjured them up in your mind, you leave room for the Spirit to work on your heart—as you recognize that there a lot of different ways that missionaries get called home.

For some, they will be called back to their homelands of where they were first called out and set apart as a missionary. And for others, they will be called home to the heavens to rule and reign with God the Father on the other side, after they have advanced in their priesthood powers, once they have returned as endowed brothers and sisters, sons and daughters, having taken out their temple covenants. So have no fear those that are called home to go to the other side of the veil will continue serving their missions on the other side of the veil and serve as ministering angels to those on this side of the veil as we go throughout the rest of The Tribulations.

I want to make note of that because some people have in their mind that they're expecting every single missionary to come back to their house where they were first called or their home ward before The Tribulations are going to start, or before The Tribulations are over. This is a false doctrine. The truth is they were never promised that they would be called home back to Utah, Idaho, or California, or Kansas; they were promised that they would be able to complete their mortal missions, complete their mortal ministry, and then they would return home to their heavenly realm. And I witness of this in Christ's name.

Eric: Thank you, Julie. I have another couple quotes here from early prophets in the church. In one, Heber C. Kimball said, "The judgments of God will be poured out upon the wicked to the extent that our elders from far and near will be called home, or in other words the gospel will be taken from the Gentiles, and later on will be carried to the Jews." This idea of the gospel going to the Jews prior to the Lord's Second Coming is also very doctrinal, and another really important thing to understand.

Julie: It is.

Eric: Do you have more to say on that Julie?

Julie: No. Just that I know that with the mission they've given me—and I don't know the timing of it or how it intersects with the other aspects of what I'm supposed to be doing—but I do know that my mission corresponds with, connects, and correlates to working in conjunction with the Jews as well as those of the other houses and the other lineages in the house of Ephraim, as well as Dan, and all of the tribes. And so it's very, very specific when it comes to the Jews being the Lord's covenant people originally and the promises He made to them through the Abrahamic covenant. There are some very deep doctrines that are tied into this gathering of the Lord's elect, and we need to be mindful that when the Lord says gathering of the Lord's elect, he does not just mean those of the LDS faith.

Eric: Mm-hmm, good point. Here's another one from Elder Orson Pratt. He says,

> "When God has called out the righteous, when the warning voice has been sufficiently proclaimed among the Gentile nations, and the Lord says 'it is enough', He will also say to His servants, 'Oh ye my servants, come home. Come out from the midst of these Gentile nations where you have labored and borne testimony for so long a period. Come out from among them, for they are not worthy. They do not receive the message that I have sent forth. They do not repent of their sins. Come out from their midst. Their times are fulfilled. Seal up the testimony among them and bind up the law.'"

Again, we have another inspired servant of Lord who saw this day when missionaries would come home, again because realizing that they had been at it for 180 plus years, the message is not being received widely, that day that Joseph Smith prophesied of just hasn't quite happened. It's being rejected and it just seems time for a cleansing and for the Lord to do his own preaching before that great day of conversion comes along.

Julie: Right. Thank you.

     Eric. I want to witness and testify to those who are listening that we live in the last days and we are exactly where we're supposed to be right now. No matter where you are, no matter what you're doing, we can always make improved choices in different areas of our lives or better choices, but we're not supposed to beat ourselves up. We're not supposed to get down on ourselves. That shame energy comes from the adversary. I want you to take a moment to think right now where your heart is and whether or not it's tied to and in conjunction with the Lord's will; what the Lord wants is our heart. He wants a broken heart and a contrite spirit. He wants hearts dedicated to the gospel and He wants people committed to the mission of returning and helping others gather home and how do we do that?

     In order for us to be able to receive the kingdom of heaven, and even exaltation, there are certain states that we must go through in order to progress in that godly pursuit. It starts first and foremost with having a heart that is turned to Christ. It is a heart that is softened, that is full of love, and that it has nothing but light that wants to be able to penetrate the hearts of others.

     In order for us to return to Father in Heaven, we must be charitable, even have the gift of charity, which can only come from Christ. It is a true gift. It's required of us in order to advance to be able to secure a place in the heavens, and that light and knowledge comes line upon line, precept upon precept, as we help others open and heal their hearts. I witness of this— we do not need to be afraid of what our station is in life, where we are, what we're doing, or what our loved ones are doing. We don't need to be worrying. We need to have faith and hope in the gospel of Jesus Christ and we need to be able to have a contrite heart and an open spirit ready to be willing and open to what the Lord would have us learn at any given moment.

We are all on our own paths to perfection. That doesn't mean we're perfect, it means we're working towards that to become like Him. It is only through Christ, through the atonement, and through God's grace that we can ever be perfected anyway. We don't need to be nervous that we have loved ones who have fallen astray or that have made mistakes. The atonement is infinite and eternal and I truly believe that when it's time for someone on their path to turn to Christ or to be perfected in Him, they will do so as we do everything we can in our power to be the best we can be. And there's no reason for us to have fear or anxiety or shame. We can have a remembrance of the things that we do wrong so that we can repent of them. That's important, but that's far different than carrying shame energy around or shaming other people and being judgmental.

Eric: Thanks for that witness, Julie. When we've talked about this great day of gathering in the future and this great conversion that takes place, again, I've mentioned this little gap or this bridge that needs to be crossed before the Tribulations. At the beginning of the Tribulations you've mentioned in your books a time when leaders of the LDS Church call out or give an invitation to gather. Is there anything that has come to your mind that might relate to missionary work or the future with regard to this call to gather?

Julie: Yes. So we've written in the books about a few of the details of the gathering as it pertains to what I see with the LDS faith. I see other churches gathering some of their people, too, but since I am a member of The Church of Jesus Christ of Latter-day Saints, and this pertains to my specific mission and my specific life, I was shown a great deal more about the LDS faith compared to other religious groups.

My understanding is that in the spring of a year, the prophet at the time of the First Presidency of The Church of Jesus Christ of Latter-day Saints who holds that office will send out a letter to wards and stakes, and they will give directions for that to be read over the pulpit. In many cases the letter will be read. In some cases, there will be satellite broadcast for those specifically in the United States. I see this also in other countries, but I'm not going to focus on that because again, most of what I saw pertains to my local area and then branched out to those areas where I have family members and loved ones.

I see that happening in the spring of a year, and I see that there'll be about a couple of months and the majority of people leaving within the first few weeks, two, three, or four months at most, before it will be time for all of those individuals to be safely secured in different locations throughout the country, mostly in the mountain west, at which point in time I see headlines, both with my name and also with many of the church members with the Prophet in general, with headlines that say, "Mormon prophet tells members to go to the mountains," and things like that.

I see that there will be the large majority who will not go, they will not heed the call for various reasons. I see that meeting where they're in the Kansas City area the meeting that I attend, there's a six o'clock and a seven o'clock. We have ushers at the doors. We're counseled to be in our seats at least ten minutes before and they shut the doors shortly thereafter, and those that are late are not permitted into the meeting. Those that leave are not permitted back in, and it's similar to when we have a temple dedication and we watch that on a broadcast from the Stake Center.

So those that are familiar with that, you know that there's their sacred responsibility to that. Obviously, there are those that leave early, that are not going to have anything to do with it. They think it's a crazy idea. Others that don't have spouses that come, maybe one partner comes, the other one doesn't, they go home and one of their family members doesn't understand. They don't want anything to do with it. There's a whole broad spectrum, an array of how people react to it, and in the large majority of the cases, if you were to take a ward of, you know, 350 people, you get maybe 2 to 10% of those individuals that will actually attend the meeting, probably about 10% actually attend the meeting, and maybe 2 to

10% that actually heed the call and actually go and gather when the prophet warns them that they should do so.

So I see members later on deciding afterwards, like when there's a big earthquake in Utah and some of the other things start to happen, that it was a foolish choice not to go, and they then try to leave on their own with their families and their loved ones to try to get and find some of those camps and locations. Some people do make it although a large majority do not. They are intercepted by volcanoes, tornadoes, tsunamis, a myriad of other things like mudslides and natural disasters; broken highways, lack of gasoline, no food, or the foreign troops actually get a hold of them.

So again, my warning voice goes out that if you're listening to this within the sound of my voice wherever you may be that you listen and that you pay attention that this the gathering of the Lord's elect and that the time will soon come that an issue will be sent out from the Prophet and you need to heed the prophet at all times. This for your safety. We've been promised that as we do so, we find safety and refuge from the storm and I encourage you to do so.

I want to confirm and let everyone know in case there is any doubt in anyone's mind where I stand on the issue. I one-hundred-percent support the prophet of the Church of Jesus Christ of Latter-day Saints, and the First Presidency and Quorum of the Twelve Apostles. I know them to be men of God. I know that the Prophet who issues this call was foreordained to do so, and while he might take some heat for it, he actually is preparing for this mission, and I know that he knows it, and he'll be able to do this perfectly when the time comes despite the criticism that comes his way.

Eric: Thank you for that witness, Julie. On another note and, as I look toward the future in this prophecy by Joseph Smith, do you see a day when Joseph's prophecy is fulfilled and the world really is filled with those who serve the Lord and love him and live his gospel?

Julie: I do. I see this prophecy being fulfilled within six years—the beginnings of it—within six years' time. I believe that we will see the beginnings of this prophecy being fulfilled; not the complete, but I see the beginnings of the prophecy being fulfilled, meaning I see the 144,000 going out in short order and beginning to preach, and thousands and thousands and thousands of people convert to the gospel of Jesus Christ. Just in the Rexburg area, San Pete Valley, and St. George area's alone there will be about a million people in each of those valleys.

Eric: Julie, that's all I have on this subject. Is there anything you'd like to add?

Julie: Well, I want people to hear very clearly that the Lord loves them, that He wants nothing more than to bring them home to safety and to help them in any way that He can to help them on their journey into their eternal progression, and he does this in a number of ways; often by letting us struggle through the daily challenges that we have so we can learn and grow and develop the qualities that make us more like Him.

I am grateful for the trials and tribulations that I've been through or will go through. I'm grateful for the heartaches. I'm grateful for the pain. I'm mostly grateful for the atonement of Jesus Christ. Without it, I would be nothing and because of it I can be everything the Lord's has promised me I could become. The same goes for each of those within the sound of my voice wherever you may be.

God is our strength and I witness to you that as we find strength in Him, we can overcome whatever trial we are experiencing, or will experience, now and forever. I witness to you that He will succor us in our time of need and that nothing is too great for our God. I witness to you that because of the Plan of Salvation, we have a plan of happiness. The infinite and eternal truths and the doctrines found in the gospel of Christ are for our good. Because of these doctrines, these laws and ordinances, we can become that which the Lord has designed us to become, which is a divine son and daughter of a loving Father in Heaven who knows far better than we do who we are and what we're capable of.

As you remember this, when we put our faith and trust in Him, we can be better than we could have ever been on our own and better than we ever imagined. I leave this witness with you, and I want to thank you Eric for all of the work that you put into these podcasts, and I hope that everyone has a wonderful day.

Eric: Thanks, Julie.

THE DAVIDIC SERVANT

EPISODE 36

Julie: Hi, welcome to the Julie Rowe Show. Today is Tuesday, September 12, 2017. Eric and I are on the line and we'd like to welcome you to our show. Eric, would you like to introduce our topic for us?

Eric: Sure. Looking forward to this one. Julie, as you and many of your listeners know, the Davidic Servant is a topic of increasingly popular discussion in certain circles. I find it an interesting topic; it's not one I've studied as in-depth as others, but I've asked myself why this is such an increasingly popular topic. Don't you think, Julie, that lots of your listeners may not even know what this is. It's not a real popular or widely discussed topic, right?

Julie: Right, right, although I've had several people asked me in the last three years and I've had, increasingly so in the last couple months' people asking about the Davidic Servant.

Eric: Right.

Julie: But yeah, I wouldn't say it's a common topic. You don't hear about it in church meetings in the LDS Church. Very few people talk about it, really because there's so little known about it.

Eric: Right, well and I've asked myself, "why is it that we don't know that much about it?" The more I study the gospel, especially with regard to these Latter-day topics, and as we transition from the Telestial Kingdom into a Terrestrial sort of Kingdom, I'm starting to understand that there are many of these doctrines that are little understood and little discussed.

The Brethren, meaning the quorum of the Twelve Apostles and the First Presidency, have said little to nothing on some of these topics. And I'm thinking well, we are in a Telestial Church, and so I'm starting to think of these other doctrines that are seldom if ever discussed as Terrestrial doctrines and therefore I find it interesting that they're, you know, becoming of interest at this time as we transition between the two kingdoms. What do you think?

Julie: Right, I agree with you on that. I find it interesting that we're at this point in history; it seems that more and more people are taking interest in some of these doctrines. I know that's not coincidental. I don't think it's that the Brethren don't want to talk about them; it's that the Lord is instructing them to talk about Telestial doctrines because the large majority of the people on the earth are still not even able to accept Telestial doctrines.

Eric: Mm hmm.

Julie: And the Lord doesn't want to give us information we're not ready for because that goes to our condemnation rather than our exaltation. So, keeping that in mind - and I'm going to be very careful with this in discussing the Davidic Servant - I've been given strict counsel from the Lord to be very cautious in what I say and how I say it, because those who are listening, once you receive this knowledge and then you take that to the Lord for a confirmation from the Spirit you are then receiving greater light and knowledge, for which you are accountable.

So, keep that in mind as you listen to this, or any other podcast that we do. Especially those that talk about doctrines that have been revealed through the Prophet Joseph Smith, and through the scriptures, but maybe have not been expounded upon. I'm not talking about new information, but I am talking about information that's not widely known, so it will seem new to many people. I want to make that clear; this not new information. There are sources out there which can serve as witnesses to my witness, but just keep in mind that these are not that widely known. The instruction I was given and very clear vision Saturday, this past weekend, was that this next podcast was to be done regarding the Davidic Servant.

I first had people asking me through email and at my speaking events, what I knew about the Davidic Servant three years ago. For the first year to year and a half my answer to them was that the Lord told me that was too sacred of a topic to discuss at the time; in part because I wasn't comfortable with my understanding of it and how that played into my mission, and I wasn't comfortable with sharing my witness until I had a sure knowledge. At that time, I was still trying to discern what I was remembering, and what the Spirit was telling me, and making sure that I was not being deceived on this topic. I can now say that I have a sure witness of some of this topic and I'm still seeking further light and knowledge regarding all of it.

Eric: Well, that sounds good. I want to hear from you in a minute what you understand. I think a good place to start is what very little we have in the scriptures. There's some stuff in Doctrine &Covenants that references this topic. There's stuff in Isaiah and other books of the Old Testament, but even before all that, I want to start in a place where most people probably wouldn't on this topic, and it's in ancient Israel culture.

If you go back to ancient times the Hebrews, our ancestors, lived the gospel in a slightly different way than we do. They lived in what we would call a Church State today. So, their government was their church, their church was their government. They had three governing functions in their society. And the first of which we would call a civic leader, or a King. The second would be the priests - you might think of the High Priest, the one who oversaw rites and rituals concerning worship, and temple, and animal sacrifice, and those sorts of things. The third was an interesting group. And to me this group is interesting for lots of reasons, but it's the group they would refer to as prophets, teachers, warners, and messengers. I think this is really important to understand for lots of reasons, even beyond the Davidic Servant.

For example, I think members of the church and others today struggle with the idea of a prophetess and what she does, and because we don't have those today in church government. Some people struggle with the idea of Ruth; "what do I do with Ruth, Deborah, Anna, or all these other prophetess as mentioned in the Bible?" The reason they fit in is in this third group of government. So, to an Israelite they would have looked to any three of those different people as a leader and they would have listened and heeded their advice and their warnings, and so forth.

Now that's an interesting place to start when we're talking about the Davidic Servant. When we hear about the Doctrine of Davidic Servant we may tend to think of it as an individual person, and that may or may not be true. What I'm learning about the Davidic Servant is that it probably is one person, but what the Spirit keeps cautioning *me* about is not to limit myself to one person as there could be many, and there could be this idea of presidencies. In other words, you have a King, like in ancient Israelite times, a Priest, and a Prophet. Okay, now I've just kind of laid some doctrinal framework and taken us back to our Israelite roots. Julie, does anything come to your mind as we talk about this idea of a governing structure or governing body?

Julie: Yes. Thank you Eric, I appreciate you laying the groundwork for that, as I come in as a witness, to let those who are listening hear the truth that I have come to understand. And then I'll let you know what I know.

First of all, what comes to mind is, as those that have listened to the radio shows and podcasts have heard me say before that the Lord works in sacred patterns. The eternities are patterned after sacred patterns. What I know, what I remember, and what I've been shown is that we have patterns of both men and women that stand in counsels and in presidencies. So, with that, my understanding here on the Earth is it's patterned the same way. The Lord works in sacred patterns. Those are eternal patterns in the Heavens. The Light side works on these patterns, the dark side simply counterfeits them, mimics, or tries to manipulate them in a manner that is not in keeping with the Lord's ways.

So, keeping with the sacred patterns of eternity, knowing that there is a presidency, essentially, we have the Godhood, which is a presidency. Here on Earth, in the Lord's church, we also have a presidency with the prophet of the church and his two counselors, and then with the councils, similar to the councils in heaven, where you have the initial twelve and then extending out into the seventies.

What I see in the councils in heaven is a council of twelve with the presidency making it fifteen, leading to a council of twenty-four, and then extending out into the seventies, and on out to a hundred and forty-four thousand more. That's the same pattern that's here on the Earth or that will be on the Earth when the Church of the Firstborn is brought to light. The Church of the Firstborn will be brought back to this Earth through the prophet, Enoch.

What happens with that is that those from the other side of the veil at a certain designated time in the plan will come to the Earth as resurrected or translated beings and they will set apart those who are serving in the presidency, working with the Davidic Servant. The Davidic Servant is a king and he has a brother who is the priest. Then there will be a Hopi Indian who will be a prophet, and there will be others that will fill the role as prophets, but in this particular instance this is a Hopi Indian. And then we have the Davidic Servant's friend who serves as a witness. That is the pattern that was established on the Earth during the days of Christ, and before Christ, including previous dispensations.

We are currently in the Sixth Dispensation, which is the dispensation of the gospel for the last time, or the dispensation of the gathering of the elect from the four corners of the Earth, and the establishment of Zion, also called the dispensation of Israel. So, keeping with these patterns I want to bring to mind different scriptures in John, in the first chapter. Now, some may ask where I learned of this, and I will say I learned of this through the Spirit, through my near-death experiences that I've had, and through confirmations of what they've been showing me regarding my mission and that of others. I have learned firsthand from John, and I think this is fitting given that there are examples in the first chapter of John in the New Testament.

If you go to John first chapter, go to verse 19 and start reading till about verse 25 or 26 and you'll learn some more about that. John the Baptist was what is considered the *Hidden Portion* of the presidency. He came as a witness of the Savior Jesus Christ prior to Christ's coming and fulfilling His mission. That was during the Fourth Dispensation presidency, so we have Peter, James, and John who are a type and shadow coming down as Prophet, Priest, and King. Then what most people don't realize, which has not been recorded, or has not been noticed, or has not been qualified, is the role that there is a fourth member of the presidency serving as the witness.

So, let's break this down a little bit; there are some patterns that occur. The king is always an archangel. The priest and king are always taken in the same manner; they're either translated or martyred. The priest and king are always related by blood; they're father, son, brothers, half-brothers. So, in this case the Davidic Servant is the King, meaning Jesus Christ. His brother, which is the priest, is John the Beloved. The Prophet is a Hopi Indian, which I don't have permission from the Spirit to disclose that person's name. And Elias is a title given to the witness in the presidency, and in this case, Elias, which is a member of the presidency, and is the Davidic Servants' friend. They all together are considered *Davidic Servants*, but it's a Davidic Servant Presidency. The Davidic King, in this dispensation of the Sixth Dispensation of the gathering of the elect, is Jesus Christ.

In the Seventh Dispensation, which is Enoch, we have Elias being the witness of Noah and Moses, the Prophet Joseph Smith, the Priest Elijah, and the King Enoch. If you back this up going to previous dispensations the first one being Adam and Seth, second Noah and Shem, the third Moses and Aaron, the fourth Jesus and James, the fifth Joseph Smith and Hyrum Smith, and then that leads us again into the sixth dispensation and you can follow that pattern. I encourage you to study that.

One of the ways that we know that the Church of Jesus Christ of Latter-day Saints was the true church, and is the true church with the ordinances, is that it follows the patterns that have been established in the scriptures. So, look for the patterns in the scriptures when you're looking for information and understanding on these greater mysteries.

So, the dispensation that's about to come forth, but hasn't yet, is this dispensation that we talk about. So, what I see is we are we are entering in to the next dispensation of the fullness of times. We are in the dispensation of the gathering of the Lords' elect. Those of us that have been foreordained to help gather the elect have been charged with the commission to witness and testify of Jesus Christ, and of His mission, thereby helping the Lord gather His children home prior to the Enoch Dispensation which takes us into the Seventh Dispensation.

The Davidic Servant, or the King, being Jesus Christ, will later become part of the next Dispensation as an Archangel. The archangels Gabriel, Jeremiel, and Raphael, and Suriel oversee the Seventh, Enoch Dispensation. There are also archangels right now that oversee the Sixth Dispensation, but I do not have permission from the Spirit to disclose those names. After the Millennial World when everything is celestialized, then we rest for another thousand years, which really just means we're doing temple work, genealogy, and lots of healing and preparing for the great Jehovah. There will be a King of that dispensation. And that's the Dispensation of the Coming of the Great God. That is the dispensation that follows our Father in Heaven, who is Father of Father's.

All right Eric, do you have any comments or questions about that? I'm not sure if I'm explaining it very well.

Eric: I think you've explained it really well, Julie. I got interested a while ago when you were talking about the book of John. If it's okay with you, I'm interested in reading those verses because I think it illustrates an important point about the understanding that Jews had about those presidencies and what they were looking for and what they weren't looking for.

Julie: I think that's great. That would be terrific.

Eric: Okay. It goes back to John 1:19-25. As I started this podcast I was talking about the way ancient Israelites knew to look for a Civic Leader, a Priest, or a Prophet. They seem to be a little less familiar with this fourth idea that Julie just introduced as *the witness*, and here's evidence. Okay, so remember John the Baptist is baptizing, and the Jews approach him and they're trying to figure out who he is.

So here we go: *"And this the record of John, when the Jews sent priests and Levites from Jerusalem to ask him who art thou? And he confessed, and denied not; but confessed I am not the Christ."* Or, in other words, I'm not the King. Okay verse 21. *"And they asked him what then? Art thou Elias?"* If you read the scriptures, then you'll know Elias was the one who oversaw those priesthood functions of the rites and rituals of the temple ordinances. So, in other words, *the Priests*. *"And he saith, I am not. Art thou that prophet?"* So, they went to the third category that they are familiar with - *the Prophet's*. So it's like they said in effect, "Okay, you're not the king, you're not the priest, then are you the Prophet?"

Julie: Which is different right? To be a prophet means we have the gift of prophecy. But to be a *Dispensation Prophet* means you hold the keys to that dispensation, in a presidency.

Eric: Right. Okay. "*And so John answered to them, No. and said they unto Him, who art thou?*" Right, so he didn't pass the test. He wasn't the King, he wasn't a Priest, he wasn't a Prophet. Verse 22: "*They said unto Him who art thou? that we may give an answer to them that sent us. What sayest thou thyself? He said, I am the voice of one crying in the wilderness, Making straight the way of the Lord, as said the Prophet Esaias.*" So, in other words, what was he saying? He was saying he was the *Witness* of those other three.

Julie: Right and *Elias* is a title given. So, there was an Elias at the time that he was asking about it, but then there's an Elias which is a title given to one who fills this role.

Eric: Right, so, there you have the Jews who were looking. They knew to look for one of those three, and were just a little confused about what the purpose and the function of a *Witness* in these sort of Dispensation Presidencies.

Julie: Right and I want to make note too, that here was John the Baptist sent forth as prophesied, but who was the hidden portion that was hidden from the world. They didn't know who he was. They were not comfortable, a lot of them - Pharisees in particular - were not comfortable with the role that he was playing, and why he would take upon himself to come to prepare, or to *claim* to prepare the way for the Christ. And yet, we know from scripture that before Mary became with child with Christ, before she became pregnant with Him the Angel Gabriel, who is the archangel of the Seventh Dispensation, he came to Mary and told her that she was going to be taken up in the Spirit and become pregnant with the Christ child.

At the same time an angel appeared to Mary's cousin, Elizabeth, and told her that she would be pregnant with John the Baptist. Both of them were given the names that they were supposed to name their sons, and they were in the same family line. That's also important that they were in the same family line, that they were on the Davidic line, and that there was an understanding there with how the patterns work related to that. So, I think it's important that we note that at that time the angel Gabriel was the one that came, and he will come *again* to fulfill his mission as the Elias in the Seventh Enoch Dispensation, after the Gathering Dispensation is complete.

So, the Davidic Servant is a descendant on the Davidic line. That's different than the Prophet David who will sit on the throne of God in Jerusalem preparing the way for the Savior to come there. There's been some confusion for some people that it's the same person. There is a prophet that I see that will go to Jerusalem, sitting upon the throne to prepare and wait during the war of Armageddon while in Jerusalem, preparing the way and preserving that seat for Christ. Then there is also Christ who serves as one of the Davidic Servants. And then there is *another*, who serves as king, as well, and those that serve as the Davidic Servant's friend.

So it gets a little bit confusing. I'm purposely not laying it out there for people because I don't have permission from the Spirit to do that. I just want to get your mind turning. I want you to think about who these servants are in this presidency. This is something you take to the Lord, and if He wants you to know it because you're ready for it, He'll explain it to you. He will even give you the names of the individuals, and He will even give you the archangel names, if that's something that He sees fit and you asked for. But, the way that the Lord works is He wants us to study it out in our minds when it comes to these mysteries of the kingdom. It's not advantageous for me or anyone else to explain it all to you because then we're not learning by the Spirit, we're basically being spoon-fed and I don't think that's how the Lord wants us to learn.

Eric: Mm hmm

Julie: Do you have anything else to say on that? Or should we go on?

Eric: No, let's, let's go on.

Julie: Okay. So tying this in and how does this affect the Church of the Firstborn? What I see with the Church of the Firstborn is that Enoch will come from the other side of the veil, along with others who will serve in this Dispensation Presidency. They then will bring to light the Terrestrial doctrines of the Church of the Firstborn and they will bring that to the Earth in what will still be a Telestial world, but as we transition from Telestial to Terrestrial, they will bring these Terrestrial doctrines to light and will establish the Presidency.

They will set the presidency apart and then that presidency will go forth and establish, identify, and set apart the hundred and forty-four thousand which will go out to preach the gospel to all the world. At that same time, we have the return of the lost ten tribes coming forth, and some of those hundred and forty-four thousand are some of the Lost Tribes that go forward.

We have those that are the Elders of Israel - this after the Thirteen Month War has ended. I don't know exactly how long after but it's not much time. We have a Thirteen Month War and it's within a year to two years after the end of the Thirteen Month War that the First Presidency of this dispensation for the Church the Firstborn is established as the Davidic Servant presidency comes forth. That happens, the hundred and forty-four thousand are called, they start being set apart, they go out, and the meetings at Adam-ondi-Ahman proceed.

Then, right around this time, or shortly before that, is the New Madrid. So, we have a big earthquake up the center of the United States going on, and other disasters going on in the world. After that the Madrid happens. After the war's over, after they're set apart and Adam-ondi-Ahman happens, then the Saints start to go from the west back to the center of the country, to the area that will soon be at that time, within a few years, beginning the establishment of New Jerusalem. That's the pattern that I see, as the patterns in the Heavens are always organized and conducive to those patterns that abide by Law and Order.

As I see it, those Davidic Servants, are called out and then *they* travel and do missionary work as well as they oversee both from a church standpoint and a political standpoint the gospel going forth, to be able to establish the Cities of Light. Eric, do you have any questions on that?

Eric: I do. I want to bring out my inner fourth grader and say, have you seen the Servant Julie? And I'm kind of wondering, does this Servant have an office or somewhere they work from?

Julie: I have seen the Servant, and they do have an office. And they have an office in the west. I'm not going to tell you where it is but there is an office in the west near where the church headquarters will be at that time. Well, we know that church headquarters will be in Rexburg, so I'm not going to tell you exactly where it is but it will be in the Rexburg area.

Eric: Okay, interesting.

Julie: I see that the Dispensation Presidency, the Davidic Servants, or the Presidency, will have offices near the church headquarters, which later will be in Rexburg after the big earthquake, but this a few years later, after that; Two or three years later after that big earthquake happens in Utah. So, I don't know the exact timeframe. Then after they have been established and the hundred and forty-four thousand begin to go out, the remaining work will be done where they are traveling the Earth as resurrected or translated beings. They will go over to New Jerusalem and help establish some of the work in New Jerusalem, preparatory to the Savior's return. Then, at a later point, they will all be living in the New Jerusalem as a City of Light.

Eric: Okay, now Julie I want to ask about this Davidic Presidency, if you will. Are there many of these kinds of Davidic Presidencies? Is there one? Or are there other councils?

Julie: There's one Davidic Presidency, but they have a council of both men and women, and then from there, more councils are set up.

That's the pattern: multiple councils, with councils overseeing councils.

Eric: Okay

Julie: That's how you can manage a hundred and forty-four thousand people.

Eric: Right.

Julie: Eric, thank you so much for your questions today. I appreciate those who are listening today, I hope it's been insightful. I don't pretend to know all of this you guys. I'm still getting bits and pieces of understanding, as far as what the missions and roles are of these individuals, but I do have a strong witness and a sure knowledge that they do work in a presidency, that there is a Davidic King and Queen; that there are individuals who work together to facilitate the mission, and that the hundred and forty-four thousand are called of God to preach to all the world, as this has been ordained of God as patterns in heaven and as we see in the temples of the Church of Jesus Christ of Latter-day Saints.

    I leave this witness with you, telling you and testifying to you so these are doctrinal truths that have been revealed. They're just mysteries of God that are not really available to the common public. I hope that by witnessing and testifying to you a little bit of what I know, this will kind of spur your own research that will cause you to ask questions of the Lord as to who you are, what your mission is, where you're going, and what the Lord has planned for *you* as you seek to find out your true identity, your divine nature, your divine role and your foreordained missions and orchestrations that the Lord has in plan.

    I'm thankful for the gospel of Jesus Christ. I have a sure witness of Jesus Christ. I love Him with all of my heart. I know that He is our elder brother. I know that He is our God and I know that He loves us with all of His heart. I have a sure witness that He does everything He can to help heal us, to comfort us, and to bring us home; that we're never given any more knowledge than we can handle. If you heard this and it's not making sense to you, don't stress out about it. Listen to it again and again if you need to, but if the Spirit tells you that it's not time for you to worry about this, then don't worry about it. This is something that comes as the Spirit directs you and teaches you when you're ready for it. And I say the same thing about anything we discuss on these podcasts or anywhere else.

The Lord wants to impart all of His goodness to us. But He doesn't want us to be fear ridden. He doesn't want us to be overwhelmed, and He doesn't want us to be condemning ourselves because we aren't ready for information. So, as you seek His face, as you seek His testimony, and witness that He's given us, you will find your own.

I leave this witness with you, my testimony again, of a sure knowledge that we have a loving Father in Heaven. We have a brother who has atoned and sacrificed for us, and that through Him all things are made possible because we can return home. We are in the Dispensation of the Gospel for the last time, or the Dispensation of the Gathering of the Elect. We are in this dispensation, our mission is to help gather the children home, on both sides of the veil. And with that I leave my witness and testimony to all within the sound of my voice saying to you: turn to Christ. It is He whom you need to seek so that you can find answers to the deepest mysteries of the kingdom. I leave this with you in the name of Jesus Christ. Amen.

Eric: Thanks Julie.

FOUNDING FATHERS

EPISODE 37

Julie: Hi. Welcome to the Julie Rowe Show. Today is Thursday September 14th of 2017. I'm here with Eric Smith getting ready to do another podcast and we hope that you find this enlightening today. Eric, welcome. Would you like to introduce our topic?

Eric: Sure. Thanks Julie. As I've read your books, and many have read your books and other near-death experience books, there's a recurring theme and pattern. Many people who have gone to the other side have had experiences where they've met and learned more about the Founding Fathers of our country, and you've described them at length in your books. I find your accounts of them to be pretty riveting. I want to ask you first, why you think this is a pattern that comes up in people's near-death experiences?

Julie: Wow! Well, I can't speak for other people. I can just speak for myself and what I understand has happened when I had my near-death experiences. It makes sense to me that with what they've shown me, they would show other people, at least in part. Each near-death experience from what I understand is tailored to that individual and their specific eternal path, like what their progression is, and what their understanding is, so if they have a specific mission, which each of us do, then they might be shown something about Founding Fathers so they can come back and witness and testify or explain some of what they understand about the Founding Fathers.

That's certainly the case for me. I met several of the Founding Fathers and I made a commitment, or was reminded when I had that experience, that I had made a premortal commitment as part of my mission to come to the earth at this time, and witness and testify about the Founding Fathers. The importance of Christopher Columbus and other developments that led to the Founding Fathers establishing the Constitution of the United States of America, and leading us into where we are currently with the state of the union. So I don't know if that answers that for you?

Eric: Yeah. I guess the question is, why do you think the Lord has seen fit to bless you with the experience of meeting those men on the other side of the veil?

Julie: Well, for one I know that my role later on is to help with the Elders of Israel as we combat the enemy forces and bring to light some of the fight against the constitution, and then put the Constitution back where it needs to be, as we prepare the way for the second coming of the Savior. So it makes sense to me that they would show me past, present, and future related to the wars in this country, or in the world, as well as the way that the Constitution was established. And reminding me of my premortal connection and relationships and friendships with some of the Founding Fathers, specifically George Washington, James Madison, John Adams, and Thomas Jefferson; those are some of the main ones that I remember from my near-death experience. There was a group of probably thirty different early settlers; men that helped to establish the Constitution that I met, but those were the leaders that I talked to.

Eric: I see. You know, there's an account going around on the internet of George Washington, who apparently had visions. When you said that it would make sense the Lord would show you some past, present, and future concerning our country, I was reminded that George Washington had seen the future of the country that he was starting to help establish. Do you believe that George Washington had those visions of the future?

Julie: I know that he did. At least some of them. I don't know if he saw everything I saw, but I know that he had several of them. I was shown the exact vision that he described about the angel coming to him, and it was given to me through George Washington's experience, so, I know he saw that. That was witnessed to me through the Savior, and through the Spirit more than once. I do know that he was a man of God. While not a perfect man, he has, and still leads armies for the light on the other side of the veil. He did that premortally before he came to earth as one of the Founding Fathers, before he led the armies here on the earth, in the United States, and he is still doing that on the other side of the veil.

Eric: I've always thought it was interesting that George Washington was in such a critical position in the establishment of our country. He ruled as the president, for two terms as I understand, and when he was done he just walked away and went to his humble home in I think it was Virginia, I can't remember exactly where, but he had a lot of opportunity. A lot of tyrants and people who would have been in that situation would have used it to their advantage to become a powerful dictator. And so it seems to be a tribute to the kind of person he was. Can you vouch for the character of George Washington?

Julie: Absolutely, I can in fact. I know him to be a High Priest in the church now. He had his temple covenants and his endowment taken care of and he's been sealed to his wife as well by proxy. He was foreordained to be a High Priest. You don't have a man like that become a High Priest who isn't a man of God, who accelerates in the priesthood on the other side of the veil like I see. There's a lot more to what goes in to George Washington when you're talking about probations and things like that.

What I understand about George Washington is that he was foreordained to come to the earth during the times when the United States was just forming because of what a valiant spirit he was in the premortal realm because he had accomplished great things in behalf of the Lord, and for the Lord, and on the light side. And so while not a perfect man, because he was mortal, his spirit is definitely one of light and goodness.

Eric: I've always just believed him to be someone who just really valued liberty, freedom, and I would say in a more spiritual term that we use - agency - he was one who fought for agency in premortality. It seems like he would be a natural fit for somebody to establish a free country like ours.

Julie: Absolutely! He was one of the great warriors for it premortally who fought in the war in heaven against the great dragon - the dragon being Satan. As the war was ensuing, and many, many people decided that they either didn't understand or didn't want to accept the Plan of Salvation as outlined, and explained, and taught to us in premortality. George Washington was one of those leaders that stood for righteousness even then.

Eric: Interesting. So, you've talked about meeting with the Founding Fathers on the other side, if there were a message today that they would give us if they were here now - and when I say *us* I mean US citizens - what do you think they would want us to know?

Julie: Well, I wrote about this in the book on page 69 of *A Greater Tomorrow* in the section titled *The Founding Fathers*. I may read some excerpts from that in a minute, but I want to speak freely of what I remember. Right before I went into essentially what was called the library, I was out in like a - it wasn't a patio, but it was out in like a corridor or garden area and sitting on a bench was George Washington, John Adams, and Thomas Jefferson. Gathered around them was a crowd of men still wearing uniform that looked like the time of the Great Revolution. John introduced me to a couple of men on the steps of that library that were wearing white robes. We walked over to the group of soldiers, and I was introduced to them, but it was like a reintroduction. I already knew them. I was familiar with all of them. It was made known to me that they were old friends. We embraced, we talked, we laughed, and we joked.

And then it got very, very serious. When it got serious, George Washington was the voice for that. John Adams spoke up and so did Thomas Jefferson. They charged me with basically remembering to come back and speak of the importance of the Constitution and the importance of agency more than anything else. The main topic was on the importance of agency. Those gentlemen that were there, those soldiers had given their lives for the Constitution and had given their lives for the freedom of this country, and although they recognized that it was part of the plan that things would turn the way they have prior to the Tribulations, they wanted to make sure that I knew, and I remembered, that they had lost their lives; and that this was no small matter; that they had covenanted premortally with the Lord to do so; that they had fulfilled their missions. And they wanted to make sure that I fulfilled mine, because of the importance of my mission that would take place once I got back.

I did promise them, and I told them that I would come back to the earth, that I would remind people of the great men that they are, that I would witness and testify to the world wherever they may be and to anyone within the sound of my voice, that George Washington, Thomas Jefferson, James Madison, John Adams, and the other Founding Fathers had acted by inspiration, and had had angelic beings minister to them to give them the words to be written in the Constitution. I was committed. And I did commit, and I commit myself now to witness and testify to the world that this true. This document came directly from the Lord, under His instruction, through ministering angels. They had ministering angels help them in the writing of the document, and they had ancestors from the other side of the veil working as guardian angels to help guide them, and to keep the adversary at bay.

I was shown scenes about the Declaration of Independence being written up and signed, and the Constitution, and the Bill of Rights, and I've been shown them several times - I don't know how many over the course of 13 years, I've probably been shown that scene and that room 50 times or something - and every time I see it, they also show me what was going on, on the other side of the veil with some of the spirits that were surrounding them, and the warfare that was going on outside of that room in order to keep the dark entities from preventing the Founding Fathers from accomplishing the work that they had been sent to do. There was literal warfare going on, on the spiritual front in mass amounts, and the same thing happened with the actual war when George Washington was leading the troops.

Anyone who studies history knows that it was an absolute miracle the war was won. I mean, by all accounts that shouldn't have happened, right, if you look at the mere numbers and the amount of provisions that we had. I look at it as a type and shadow for what's going to happen now with the Elders of Israel as we fight enemy forces. Those enemy forces including the US government and the troops that'll be against us, by all accounts are much more advanced in their skill level. They're much more advanced. They have the provisions, they have the money, they have the weapons, and the Elders of Israel and those that work with them will be at odds.

They will be against them. And they will be outnumbered physically and from weaponry, but they will have the powers and priesthoods of God, and the angels on the other side of the veil to help protect them, to help guide them, to inspire them, and to help give them priesthood power to be able to combat enemy forces on both sides of the veil, and I see the same thing having happened in the Revolution.

Eric: That's a really scriptural pattern for the Lord to do that. It happened in the Book of Mormon.

Julie: Yes.

Eric: It happened in the Bible where he starts with a large army and whittles it down to just a few righteous men, and then they...

Julie: Right, there's a reason in the first book that I also talked about the stripling warriors. The passages that I selected and put in the books, especially the stories from the Bible and from the Book of Mormon were specifically chosen. John gave me those passages. He told me what to write. He told me how to write them. And I was inspired, and every time I would go to write something different, to add details that I saw that were more exciting, or would give more information, I was told to keep it simple; keep it basic, in part because nobody would believe that I'd actually seen that stuff and it was too much for people.

So it was really hard when I wrote the books, because I wanted to expound. I wanted to like say everything I saw in my head. And I was forbidden by the Lord to do so because I was told to keep it on a fourth-grade level for people, and that means on a doctrinal and a reading level so that an average adolescent or teenager could read the book, or somebody who had never been exposed to the gospel at all could read the book and gain understanding on a gospel perspective.

Eric: Interesting...

Julie: I find it fascinating. I was just thinking I should go back and read my book. I haven't read my book since I wrote it 2014, and I think it would be interesting to go back and read it now with the perspectives I have now, and the understanding I have now about my mission, and about where we are three years later.

Eric: You should. That leads, and prompts the question: Have you had additional insights since your near-death experience pertaining to the Founding Fathers?

Julie: Absolutely! I keep getting visions of them on the other side of the veil. They each are in charge of armies on the other side of the veil. Spiritual armies. I see George Washington as a master general. He is basically a master general who is leading the troops. Joseph Smith is as well as Noah and Moses; they have their stewardships. And the Founding Fathers, especially those who've been made high priests, have a different responsibility, kind of a higher priesthood power, over certain troops, or over certain wars there.

And then you've got those that signed the Bill of Rights. There are several of them that have taken leadership positions on the other side of the veil to help prepare the troops coming for the battles that are ahead. I see them practicing. Actually I see them working actively. And I see them practicing for the war that's coming up. I see them lining up. I see them having face-offs as it is right now, even in Denver, or Salt Lake, and other places throughout the world.

Eric: Can you help those of us who aren't as visually inclined as you, or who have seen those sorts of things? When you say there are troops and they're lining up, I mean, what does this look like?

Julie: Like war! Literally!

Eric: Like they're holding guns, swords, weapons, or...?

Julie: Yes. Spiritual weapons. Yes. Yes.

Eric: And who is it they're fighting?

Julie: Spirits of darkness that also have weapons.

Eric: Okay. So, I'm imagining here on the earth, we may have people who are actually fighting, or going to work, and or struggling with pornography, or other addictions, or those kinds of things, and I'm imagining somewhere above my head then, George Washington and his troops going against dark forces who are, I don't know, congressmen, and government leaders...

Julie: Or right there next to you in a different sphere, because they're all right here in just a different dimension. It's hard to conceptualize because our human minds can't do it. But, those that have a thin veil, or very little veil know that I speak the truth. That explains a lot of what we experience in our lives; everything from the miracles we experience, as well as the heartaches, the pains, the physical pains, the mental and emotional issues that we suffer from. There's a lot more that goes into this mortal existence than we understand.

Eric: Ok, so now I'm just kind of wondering to what extent do they get involved? Would there be a lineup of troops on the other side for me individually? Or would that more likely be for like a government leader or somebody who has a more important role?

Julie: Well, you have a pretty important role from what I see in the eternal perspective right now, Eric. So, I see armies defending you, as we speak, outside of your home for us to be able to do this podcast recording. I live on 20 acres and I've got millions of fighters that are constantly on my property defending the space that I live in. Even at that, there are some that are allowed to enter in, or that sneak in, or come in through cracks and crevices, and shields are broken. But for the most part, I would not be alive were it not for the defense of the priesthood power on the other side of the veil.

Eric: Wow.

Julie: I don't believe you would be either. They intervene far more than we know, and that is their job. We have the warrior spirits on the other" side of the veil, but that is their sole job right now; to protect, to defend, and to keep at bay as they learn their powers and priesthoods and advance in their estates.

Eric: Very interesting. Well, thank you for that witness. That's touching to me. I appreciate it.

Julie: Mm-hmm.

Eric: What other sort of things did you see on the other side of the veil concerning these men and their missions?

Julie: Well, gosh it's hard to know where to go with that. Let me just answer it like this. I see many of the Founding Fathers as prophets, seers, and revelators.

Eric: Interesting.

Julie: Not now, but later.

Eric: We've talked a lot about Founding Fathers; do you have any visuals or understanding concerning women who are fighting for freedom on the other side of the veil?

Julie: Yes. That's why I love the Wonder Woman movie (laughs); it's one of the many reasons I love it. I joke all the time that I'm truly an Amazon because I had people say that I was an Amazon when I signed up to have these guys call me an Amazon woman because I'm 5' 10-¾". I used to take offense at it. Now I think it's a compliment. If I can fight anything like those ladies, well, bring it on. I think that's terrific.

They work in a different capacity with how they actually spend warfare. There are warrior angels that are women. And then there are also women that are ministering angels, just like we have men that minister with priesthood blessings, we have women that do the same. We have women that remove the weapons and that pull them from wounds and things like that in a nursing capacity; those that are skilled in the dark arts, they all have their assignments.

They're all skilled in certain areas and being taught how to do their missions on the other side of the veil. We have recorders. We have presidents of organizations. We've got secretaries. We've got historians. Basically everything you see here on earth is like a type and shadow, or an example of what's on the other side of the veil. It's just a different realm. And you have the counterfeits of that in the dark worlds in degrees, and the degrees of counterfeit are basically based on the degrees of the spiritual darkness as you go into lower estates.

Eric: Julie, can you tell us about your experience growing up with freedom? Were you raised in a freedom-loving home? Were you taught to value our freedoms, and government, and the Constitution, and these kinds of things?

Julie: Yes. I always felt a strong calling, if you will, to agency. My dad was an LDS Chaplain in the military. He did 30 years and retired a full-bird Colonel in the United States government military, in the army, and had a unique situation because he was a Chaplain. He trained in weaponry. Although he never carried a weapon, he had a Chaplain's Assistant who carried the weapon which was essentially that guy's entire job, to protect my dad. I think that's interesting.

Because of the veil being thin for me, I see that often in my case, right? I don't carry any weapons. I've been instructed for my mission that while it's important for me to learn how to shoot, I personally am not to carry a weapon. I've got those on the other side of the veil, and those on this side of the veil who have the assignment to protect me, similar to what my dad had as a Chaplain with having a Chaplain's Assistant.

I find that really interesting because that was essentially his bodyguard and I didn't know any differently. Every time we moved, when I got a little bit older, I paid attention to who the Chaplain's Assistant was because he was the one that was going to give his life for my dad if it came to wartime. My dad was 6' 6-½", and I was always kind of sensitive about that. When he'd have somebody that was like 5'-10", you know, protecting him (laughs) I was like, they're going to shoot his head off.

So, I was raised very much so with patriotism. We went to several different functions: The chaplains' get-togethers, the brigade parties, the division parties, the picnics. I was raised where my parents taught me very well about the importance of freedom and the Constitution. Giving the Pledge of Allegiance was very important. We went to the parades. We went to the different activities they had. There was always a great deal of respect for the military and for the role that the military played, and for agency. There was an interesting mix because, as you know, coming from a military family there often can be a lot of strict rules that are kept in a family. I was raised in a very strict family - Very! I have a very dominant dad when it came to making sure that we were respectful, and that we valued hard work, and that we valued the importance of the lives that had been given for our freedoms in past times.

So from a young age, every time I remember being at school and just citing the Pledge of Allegiance and get getting teary-eyed as a young girl and not understanding, like why is this so dear to my heart, you know. I'm in third grade and I'm crying and nobody else in my classroom is crying when they give the Pledge of Allegiance; or when we would stand and watch the processions; or in high school, when I would see men in uniform and I would think about what they had been sacrificing.

I remember in Hawaii in sixth grade waking up every morning at like 6:00 or 6:30 to the infantry men and women running and singing their songs as they ran. I remember after my freshman year of college coming home and telling my dad how much I missed hearing the familiarity of the military. So it's very much ingrained in me, and it's something that was very much a part of my life. I'm very, very grateful for that upbringing. I'm thankful for the sacrifices of the servicemen and women.

Our chief isn't exactly someone that I agree with. I don't necessarily feel like we've had a president or chief of staff over the Armed Forces for a long time that I've agreed with. It's been decades since I felt like we had a president and chief of staff who actually was looking out for the welfare of our servicemen and women. In fact, I think they're doing the opposite right now where they're putting those lives on the line unnecessarily and purposefully to try to create more havoc for us in the United States. That absolutely brings me to tears when I think about the sacrifices families are making, knowing that we have a lot of corruption in the military now.

If I had my way, none of us would ever go to war, but I do know that it's part of this mortal existence; that Satan, the dragon, has committed himself to causing a war on the woman as well as on the men and women on this earth, and it makes me think about what we have right now going on with the Book of Revelation coming about on September 23rd - Revelation 12 - that the dragon will make war with the woman, and that comes into line with what I understand the Founding Fathers were asking me to do regarding my mission. That was an earful right there wasn't it?

Eric: (laughing) It was good. Thank you. I heard something yesterday on the internet. It was something like, if young people today were given the choice, they would give up their right to vote if it meant they could have their student loans cleared away. Reading that felt like an indication to me of the times we live in. How do you feel about the way we view our freedoms now days?

Julie: Well, I wouldn't be surprised, first of all, if they try to throw that out there to people, give up your right to vote and we'll wash it away; we have been absolutely brainwashed in this country. Not just with false education, false ideas, traditions, and belief systems in our school systems, and our churches, and our government, in our societies. I think it's a crying shame where we are as a nation when it comes to Common-Core and other things that are being taught in the schools.

Revisionist history has been going on in my lifetime and longer than that. We're seeing the fruits of that coming about now as we have Millennials and others who have absolutely zero credibility when it comes to knowing what's going on in this country, or what has gone on in this country. Therefore they don't have any idea who to vote for, not to vote for, what to vote for, and whether or not they even care to vote; because they don't have any skin in the game, right?

Eric: mm-hmm

Julie: They don't know anybody. Most of them have no attachments or connections to anyone who's ever served in the Armed Forces. Most of them don't pay attention to what's going on. If they're reading the news, they're getting bad news. They're getting lies. And then they're hearing stuff on social media which is just a bunch of crap. So, I know that we have a generation of Millennials coming forward now that are the most valiant spirits that have ever been on the planet and many of them will give their lives for Christ.

I know that that's what they premortally signed up to do. When the Lord gathers the elect, and he takes those children, and he puts them in the mix, if you will, when it's time, it's going to be a rude awakening for them. But it will lead to ultimate exaltation. In the meantime, it will lead to victory for those who are left to be able to bring about His eternal purposes, which is to preserve the Constitution so that we can go in, build New Jerusalem, and build up the Church of the Firstborn, and prepare the way for the Savior to come back, so he can take his rightful place as King of Kings.

Eric: Julie, a minute ago you mentioned you wouldn't be surprised if they tried to take that right away. The question that came to me was: what rights do you think they have taken away already, and do you foresee them attempting to take additional rights away from us?

Julie: Well, they tried to take about all of our rights away. The first one comes to right to privacy. They use the full freedom of speech thing. They're taking that away even as we speak. I see them taking that away explicitly in the future. If you say or do something that goes against the norm, or what they are saying the status quo is, in order to get food, clothing, shelter, and other things in the future, essentially they'll take the freedom of speech away in that manner. It's already been taken away in the news, because the news outlets are bought and sold by the puppet masters. I see definitely the right to bear arms being taken away. They're trying to take it away as we speak. I see that right to bear arms being taken away. That will have significant impact on the country.

I see the right to life being taken away as we have so many abortions going on in this nation. I just had somebody send something to me that was that was disheartening; it's another marker in the road. They had a satanic statue, and the article in the news paper in Missouri talked about how a certain organization related to parenthood in Missouri signed a deal with the Satanists and satanic cults to build more abortion clinics in the state of Missouri. The legislature passed it; the judge passed it. So I see in very real ways the right to life being taken. The good news about abortion is if someone is aborted, on the other side of the veil they do have an opportunity to go on to another estate, and to go on to another family. So it's not all over for that spirit if their life is cut short. That gives me hope because of all the babies that have had their probation cut short.

Same thing with the right to privacy. Every time I fly, which has been about once a month or every other week for three years, they have the computers that can supposedly send off a trigger if you've got some metal or something on you or you have to be patted down. I can wear the exact same outfit to the airport that I did the week before and the computer will show I'm fine one time, and it'll show that I have to have a total pat-down the next time. It's a load of crap. It's a total facade. It's a lie. Their systems are purposely wired and jacked that way. They're training the people at the airports, in the military, and other forms of government, to be suspicious, to be controlling, and to be yes-men, basically, and I just see that leading to a lot of a future corruptions and a lot of problems with control.

Same thing with our police departments, and our fire stations, and other things. We will have good men and women in the Armed Forces, and police departments, and school systems, and other forms of government that will stand to the occasion. They will rise and they will rebel against the institutions. They will rebel against the system. Many of them will lose their lives for it, but in the end it will be for their good, and for ours, as many, many, many of them will not do so and they will be part of the corrupt system that leads to everything from satanic rituals being ensued, and the death of a lot of people. So it is a very, very heavy topic for me. When I think of the Founding Fathers, I know that they would be turning in their graves, except for the fact that they too know the plan. They have hope that we can rise above this devastation that's about to come to the country.

Eric: Hmm. Interesting. Are there other things that we ought to be looking for in the near future; things to be concerned of with our government leaders and potential rights being taken away?

Julie: Yes. I'd say we need to get familiar with the Constitution. Take a look at that Bill of Rights again, if it's been a long time since you actually read through the Constitution, or read through the Bill of Rights. Point, by point, by point, you can count on them taking every single one of those away, unless we do something about it. They already are. They're already trying to. And they will be successful for a season. But we will rise up. We will raise the flag and a banner of freedom just like Moroni did in his day, and hold that banner and hold that flag. We will rise to the occasion as the Elders of Israel gather together with those from the tribes of Israel that will return, and with that we will combat the enemy forces as we have a standoff in Grand Junction, and then later in Denver before we pave the way to New Jerusalem.

I witness and testify of this. This is true; I've seen it over and over again. We just need to have faith, and courage, and be brave. We're going to have several of our men that might get shot, but, I've also seen that several of these men will come back to life. So I don't want the men and boys that are of age to go to war to be afraid. Many of you will see incredible miracles. And even if you get shot, you're going on to a better place. Or you may just be coming right back to this earth to finish out your mortal probation. So there's always an eternal plan and we just have to have faith in what that is.

Eric: Well, that should give us some hope. Thanks. That definitely gives me some hope. I think often of my forefathers. I'm a son of the American Revolution through Captain Samuel Smith who was a great-grandfather to Joseph Smith. I come through him and we have great family pride in knowing that our ancestors fought for the freedoms of our nation in the Revolutionary War. I've often wondered if I might have an opportunity to defend our freedoms like our grandfathers of old have.

I'm grateful for these men. I'm grateful for those who've gone before us and given us the freedoms we have today. I hope everybody in the sound of my voice will do what they can to look in their family histories, and look to those within your ancestry, who have helped preserve those freedoms, and honor their names, and try to continue the legacy that they passed on to you.

Julie: Thank you Eric. I appreciate that, and I appreciate what you've shared in your witness. I want to witness and testify to each of you that God loves you. That he has a plan for you that's an eternal plan of salvation and of happiness, and that through that plan we can find joy now and into the eternities. I want to witness and view of the importance of the family, the importance of calling upon our ancestors to help with the things that we are working on in our lives. To give us ministering aid, and to give us protection as we have guardian angels that will come and assist us as we ask for their help.

There is no limit to priesthood power. It's a limitless power. And as we tap into that, we are given additional shielding and protecting. I encourage you to ask the Lord about what that means, to put on the armor of God. Ask Lord how you can shield yourself enough with what you can do to better combat the enemy wherever you may be, now or on the other side of the veil.

I testify to you that God is willing to do everything he says he's willing to do; which is to fulfill all of his promises to you that he made premortally. All the promises he makes to you now. I know this to be true as I've seen in my life unfolding great miracles that I was promised 13 years ago. Some of those answers have come just this week. Things that I was shown and told about 13 years ago are now coming to fruition. In less than a week's time I have learned more about my personal identity, more about my personal mission, and it's very humbling to be at this point. I testify to you that you can know the same as you seek the Lord's face and do everything you can to call upon him and through his power to reveal to you from him the mysteries of the kingdom.

I leave this witness and testimony with you knowing that God is over all. That he loves you dearly. That we have a brother, even Jesus Christ, who has suffered and died for you. And because of that, he was resurrected. You too will be resurrected one day. You have completed your first estate. You have completed your second estate. You are here on your second estate, or have completed that second state. I witness and testify to you that this is the case. I leave this witness with you and say to you, look to God for all things, knowing that through our obedience to the gospel and to the principles of the gospel, we will understand the doctrines greater as we stick to those things which will keep us in the light and help us become whole and healthy. I leave this testimony with you in God's name. Amen.

ABRAHAMIC COVENANT
AND CITIES OF LIGHT

EPISODE 38

Julie: Welcome to the Julie Rowe Show. Today is Thursday, September 14, 2017. I've got Eric Smith on the line and we're getting ready to do another podcast. Eric, welcome.

Eric: Thanks Julie.

Julie: Eric and I have been talking about different podcast ideas. We are grateful for those that have emailed their ideas in and ultimately we decide how to do these podcasts by what the Spirit directs us to do. And so a couple weeks ago we were talking about a few different topics and then this morning decided upon the one that we're going to do this afternoon. Eric can you introduce that for us?

Eric: You bet. This was one that's been on my list to talk with you for a little while. It's the doctrine of the Abrahamic Covenant. Now the reason I feel like it's okay to talk about that on this show and, I've talked about this with Julie, is that Julie has mentioned a great deal about things in the future. When I was studying the Abrahamic Covenant a number of years ago I began to see how the Abrahamic Covenant tied in to the doctrine of the latter-days and the Tribulations and what follows those as Julie would call into the *Greater Tomorrow*.

I want to try to connect some dots for those who have studied Abraham and the latter days and see what it all means. As usual, Julie,

122

your witness is always invaluable. Please just feel free to chime in. I do have a lot of material and a lot of scriptures to walk through, but the thing that will bring it to life is your witness and your experiences as well. Does that sound okay?

Julie: Yeah, sounds great. Thanks Eric.

Eric: Okay. This journey started for me years ago as I would read The Book of Mormon each year as a tradition. I would always hit this one verse in 1st Nephi 14:17. Every time I came to this verse I would read it, scratch my head for a minute, and say "What!? That doesn't make sense." And then I would keep reading and then I would hit it the next year and I would have the same reaction for seriously, I don't know, five, six, seven years I would do this. And so finally five or six years ago I started saying myself, "What does this mean?" So let me read the verse and I'll walk you through some of what happened next.

It says, "And when the day cometh that the wrath of God is poured out upon the mother of harlots which is the great and abominable Church of all the earth whose founder is the devil," I want to pause right there and point out that I began to understand that "day" that it was talking about was the *Day of Tribulation*. I have no doubt of that. Again, when the day when the wrath of God is poured out upon the abominable church of all the earth, it says, "*then at that day* the work of the Father shall *commence* in preparing the way for the fulfilling of his covenants which he hath made to his people who are the house of Israel."

Now here's what stumped me. It said, "*Then* at *that* day," or in other words, during the Day of Tribulation or shortly after, "the work of the Father shall *commence*." Can you see what troubles me there? The word "commence" means *to begin*. So I'm thinking, wait a minute, the Days of Tribulation lie in our future. The Church of Jesus Christ of Latter-day Saints or the Lord's work has been restored. Hasn't his work already commenced?

So I had to reconcile this thought of when this great day of the Lord's fulfilling his covenants commenced? According to this verse it did not commence with the restoration of the Gospel - it will commence during The Tribulations. I find that really interesting. I want to encourage you to read this verse. It's 1st Nephi 14:17.

But then to my surprise I studied the scriptures and found (I'm counting right now 3, 4, 5, 6 ...) 11 other verses in scripture scattered throughout the Book of Mormon that use similar language about the day *commencing* following the tribulations. I was just so puzzled by that. So then the next question naturally was "well, what are the covenants then? And why do they commence during the tribulations?"

So that's the place to start with that question is by studying Abraham. Naturally we go back to the Book of Abraham, Chapter 1:1 and 2. And we need to paint the picture of what it was like where Abraham was living as when he was a younger person. He was living in Ur of the Chaldees. Which some estimate is way up north kind of in the Russia area or, possibly in Scandinavia somewhere up north. He was living in a hedonistic Society, with human sacrifice and all manner of abominations going on. But we do understand that the people in this location did have some measure of priesthood authority. It appears to have been the lesser priesthood. It's pretty clear that they did not have the higher priesthood, or Melchizedek Priesthood.

Now, to paint more of the picture of what it was like for Abraham. He would have just witnessed the City of Enoch being translated. Okay so we have a great dichotomy for Abraham. He understood what it was like to be living in a hedonistic society of murder and all kinds of terrible things, but he also knew what it was like to have a translated city; a city of people that he may have known or have heard of who were so righteous that they were taken up off the earth. We can read about that in Moses Chapter 7. He also was contemporary with Melchizedek who was another righteous man, who had a righteous city of his own and was also translated. We don't hear much about the city of Melchizedek, but we can read about that in Genesis, chapter 14. Especially the Joseph Smith translation gives us more detail.

Julie on that note I just wonder if you have any comments or witness you might add concerning these two great cities that were translated in Abraham's time.

Julie: I, do. But I don't know how much I can actually share on that other than witness and testify that they existed. I see them basically like great cities of light.

Eric: Uh-huh.

Julie: They are types and shadows of what we will see in the coming days of the Tribulations when cities of light and places of refuge are established; places of refuge, but then later become cities of light. Anyway, let's continue and go from there and we'll see where the discussion takes us.

Eric: Awesome, thanks, Julie. So again, I want to just highlight this contrast between Ur of the Chaldees where Abraham lived, and these two righteous - I might call them *Zion Societies*.

First, in Ur of the Chaldees, they were idolatrous; meaning they had many false gods. Contrast that with the Zion societies who worshiped the true and living God. Ur of the Chaldees had false priests, and did have the lower priesthood, but they were false priests who did whoredoms with their powers. It was an abomination before God.

Contrast that with these two Zion societies who had the fullness of the Priesthood, specifically the Melchizedek priesthood; the high priesthood, and they exercised it in righteousness. Ur of the Chaldees had hedonistic rituals and human sacrifice, but in the Zionistic societies of Enoch and Melchizedek, they had true ordinances, true worship, and practiced the rituals in the way that God had prescribed them to be practiced.

And lastly, an interesting point about the society Abraham lived in is he came from a broken covenant line of priesthood. In other words his father, Terah, was also hedonistic, had broken his covenants, and had apostatized. Therefore, Abraham was not connected to the father's, meaning Noah and Adam and others, because his father had broken his covenants. So Abraham had the sense that he didn't belong in the family of God because he was disconnected through the breaking of these covenants.

Contrast that with these Zion societies who all had their temple ordinances and sealing's complete. No lines were broken. They had *all things in common* among them and no poor among them. So we have this great contrast then, between those cities.

So the next thing to study is what Abraham then wanted. He had this great dichotomy of wickedness and righteousness. Abraham was a righteous person. He was repulsed by the sin that was all around him, and was very drawn to the righteousness that was in the City of Enoch and Melchizedek. In Abraham 1: 1-2 we hear what Abraham wanted through this dichotomy. And there are eight points. Let me just mention those briefly.

1. He said he wanted another place of residence, which is obvious. He lived in a dark place. He wanted to live in a light place.

2. He wanted greater happiness and peace and rest. So this tells us he wasn't restful. He did not have peace. He was not happy, or at least he had some measure of happiness and recognized there was more to be had.

3. "I sought for the blessings of the fathers and the right whereunto I should be ordained to administer the same." In other words, he recognized that he was lacking in priesthood power and authority.

4. He had great knowledge and wanted *greater* knowledge. So this again sheds light that they did have some semblance of priesthood power; of light and knowledge, but he knew there was more to be had.

5. He wanted to be a greater follower of righteousness. This tells us that he was already a follower of righteousness, but he wasn't satisfied and he sensed there was more out there, he just didn't know where it was and how to find it.

6. He wanted to be a father of many nations; a prince of peace.

7. He desired to receive *instructions*. Now that's a curious word if you study that and think about where you've heard the word "instructions" in a priesthood context.

8. He wanted to keep the commandments of God. He lived in a hedonistic, idolatrous society where there was no law. Anything goes, but he was willing to be bound by commandments and knew that those commandments would actually make him more free.

Do you have any comments up to this point Julie?

Julie: I think that's just beautiful how you've outlined it. You know, my mind keeps going back to the days of Abraham; the days of what they must have gone through. And then I just can't help but think of Christ and what He's gone through for us to help fulfill these promises. Without father Abraham, the Covenant would not have gone forth, and without Christ it wouldn't either.

Eric: Uh-huh.

Julie: I just quite honestly am humbled by what I see right now as I'm being reminded of what great men they were and are, on both sides of the veil. I don't have words to describe the visions in my head right now. Also thinking about the women that were associated with them and the friends and family members that were surrounded by them and how they must have really been challenged, and trying to understand the identity of these individuals and what it was that God was giving them, or the role that they play in the eternities.

I think that's a type and shadow for what we experience in our own day as we have those ministering to us from the other side of the veil to help us with our own identities; to help us understand our own divine nature and our roles, now and into the eternities. I'm just greatly humbled at the thought of being able to have this Abrahamic Covenant come to fulfillment in the coming days.

Eric: Thanks Julie. I appreciate your witness and I like how you've mentioned these things are types and shadows. I think that's key. I want to keep building to that point here. So, here's another type and shadow:

We move, then, into the period of Abraham's life where there are tests. First of all, I think it's important to notice that he did want to leave the place he was currently living, which was the first test. What that meant for people in this day and age was, if you left your place of residence you were walking away from your inheritance. So for us today just imagine, your father has great wealth and land possessions; if you walk away from your land of inheritance, you walk away from everything. And you have to begin again. So this was the first test of Abraham which we read about in verse one.

I find it also fascinating that he knew and sensed there were greater things to be had of God but did not know where to find them. But when the wicked priests tried to sacrifice him on the altar, Jehovah came to rescue him and said "I will take you to another place." He doesn't appear to have told Abraham where He was going to take him, and Abraham didn't appear to really understand where that was and why he was going there.

Julie: Right, he didn't, he didn't know. He went on faith from what I understand and what I remember.

Eric: See, and that's key. It makes sense that it would be on faith, because he just kind of started walking. He got some family and some possessions and went. Before long, where did he end up? He ends up at the feet of Melchizedek. Abraham talked about knowing and wanting more priesthood, and wanting more power, and wanting to be sealed to his father, and wanting ordinances and blessings, and where did the Lord take him? To one of the only people in the whole land who had those things, Melchizedek.

Sure enough, he goes to Melchizedek; receives all the blessings of the temple; receives the higher priesthood, the sealing power, ordinances, and everything that came with living in a Zion-like society.

So again, the first test was leaving his land of inheritance. He was faithful. He did it. The second test, we read about him being offered up that I just mentioned by the wicked priests. Jehovah rescues him. And the covenant-making process begins, and I say *it begins* because you find as you study Abraham's life this was not a single event, like some of us tend to think. I used to think this way, that it was just a single event; No, the Covenant-making process involved many key moments and it built and built and built until the final great covenant that we kind of talk about.

Julie: Thank you.

Eric: Yeah. Okay, now there's another test, and I have about four more to go through. Abraham then in this new land made a coalition with his nephew, Lot, and others. They basically become a city or a society, a band, a group, or a family group. They began to fight the Mesopotamian's in that land to inherit this land that he sensed was going to be the Promised Land.

The Mesopotamian King told Abraham to take all the spoils of this war that they had won with the Mesopotamians. Abraham chose not to take the spoils. He rose above worldliness and materialism. He passed this test. And so seeing that Abraham had passed that test, the Lord blessed him. That's when he actually led him to Melchizedek to receive the ordinances and all the things that he desired. You can read about that in Genesis Chapter 14.

There's another significant event here: a little test that reminds me so much of Joseph Smith. I don't actually have the reference, I need to get it, but where Abraham goes to pray. It's that experience where he takes all these animals, divides them in half, puts those animals in a line, and then Jehovah comes down, walks through those animals that had been divided in half, and makes a covenant with the Lord. But before all that happened, something really interesting occurred. He talked about this ruckus that the birds started making right before the Savior came down and walked through those animals. It was so important that it was worth noting in scripture that the birds made a big ruckus.

Well if you think back to Joseph Smith's experience right before he had the sacred experience with the Father and the Son in the Sacred Grove, the adversary came and tried to choke him and bind him and prevent him from speaking. It appears that Abraham had the same experience as these birds came and we're creating this big ruckus over all these animals that had been divided. It was obviously to try to stop this great covenant from taking place.

Julie: Uh-huh.

Eric: Then we have the test Abraham went through with his son Isaac. Abraham was told to go and take his son and sacrifice him. Now we know the story. He attempts to sacrifice him and the Lord tells him he doesn't have to. But there's so much more to that story that we don't hear, and is worth noting more of the detail of what he actually experienced in this.

Abraham was told to perform the olah sacrifice. Okay, this was a Hebrew-like ritual that we would call the *burnt offering*, and it's worth describing what this is. In the olah sacrifice, it was understood that you would take an animal and slit its throat. You would then drain the animal of all its blood into a dish that would hold that blood. You would then dismember the animal, cutting all its limbs apart removing the fat from the muscle and the bone creating different piles of those things.

You would then take, wash, and anoint the meat that had been removed and divided. You could put salt on these things and oil and that sort of thing. And then you would take every bit of it and consume it completely and entirely in flame, and it would ascend to God, leaving nothing behind. It was a *consecrated* sacrifice. For three days, as Abraham went to the land of Moriah, he had this sacrifice on his mind. I imagine him saying to himself, "How am I going to do this to my son?" It's gruesome, and he knew exactly what he was commanded to do. Yet he went, and he was faithful. So Julie, with that in mind I would like to hear what you have to say about that.

Julie: Well, in part what I see is he was commanded to do this to break the curses and the contracts that had been on his family line. He had come from a family of essentially Satanists, if you will, who had done acts like this for Satan. This was an Abrahamic test of the Lord given to him so that he could break the contracts and curses on that family line, basically through obedience to the laws and ordinances of the gospel; being willing and teaching his son, Isaac, of these covenants that they needed to make with the Lord.

He had been taught incorrectly, and then he was taught by the Lord the correct doctrines the correct principles, the correct gospel. As a test of his faith he had learned to hear the Lord's voice and he knew the difference between the two. He was trying to make sense of why this would be. The part that is not well known - because it's not written in the scriptures that we have now, although I believe records will come forth later that will validate what I say - what I saw was that Abraham had conversations with Isaac. They were both visited by angels or an angel, the angel Gabriel. They were visited by the Lord who educated them on the necessity for this. They were only given as much light and knowledge on this as the Lord saw fit, to be able to test them succinctly and adequately, to be able to fulfill the covenant that was being made.

And with that, Isaac was 33 years old. He was an active participant in this, which is a similitude of the Savior, whose mission was completed at the age of 33, so there are types and shadows in

Abraham's day with Isaac similar to what we saw with Jehovah later. The view that I had was that they walked for quite some time; several miles up a mountain and over some tenuous circumstances. Isaac carried much of the kindling that he knew was going to be used for his own sacrifice. He went willingly. This is a part of the story that is often untold which is that Isaac as a grown man, was with his father, Abraham, who at that point was very elderly. There is no way that Abraham was able to lift Isaac on the altar. Abraham told his son what had to happen, and Isaac climbed on that altar himself.

Eric: Hmm.

Julie: He allowed it to happen. And I thought during my near-death experience and in vision, what I saw was everything being done in preparation for this, and Isaac building the altar with Abraham. They built it together. They gathered the rest of the kindling together. He prepared everything for his father, who was elderly. And he prepared his own sacrifice. He was willing, similar to the Savior, in a similitude of what the Savior went through. He also was tested. With that, he laid himself down on the altar. Abraham pulled the knife out, and as he held it to Isaac's throat, then the angel Gabriel interceded. And so it was right up to the very hour. It was a test of faith for both of those men. And they passed the Abrahamic test successfully. It was an Abrahamic test for Isaac and for Abraham.

Eric: Oh, Julie, thank you so much for that witness! I love that! I love hearing more about that experience! So special.

Julie: You're welcome.

Eric: And there are two other tests. Well there are probably lots of other tests, but I have a couple more. Like one, the Lord told Abraham and his wife, Sariah, to go to Egypt. And the custom at the time was that Pharaoh in Egypt could have any woman he wanted as his wife. And so Abraham and Sarah had a pretty good understanding if they went there that Sarah would be become property of Pharaoh. It took great, great faith to go there knowing that Sariah would be given away.

Julie: Absolutely.

Eric: There was another test. For the remainder of his life the Lord had promised Abraham that he would receive certain lands and inheritances and posterity as numerous as the stars in the heavens and the sands in the sea. This last test was that he never received those things in his life. He was in the land of his inheritance, but he didn't get to see it in the state and condition that he wanted it to be, so you could say another test he had was to remain out his days in a desert, in a tent, living off bugs, or whatever it was they ate, but he sacrificed greatly and never really received the blessings that he wanted in his life. And so that would have been a great test for him as well.

Julie: Right. He did not live in mortality to see that during that probation, but he is very much a part of what's going on now, and he will yet see the Covenant fulfilled. God fulfills all his promises to his children.

Eric: Very well said. And that's kind of where I would like to culminate this podcast here in a few minutes. Go read Hebrews 11: 8-10, and it talks about how Abraham was faithful and he struggled and had trials and he "looked for a city which hath foundations whose builder and maker is God." Think of any cities you've heard described. I know Julie has described cities like that in her books.

Okay, next I think it's important to discuss what was covenanted. So he was promised that his posterity would be numerous, his seed and descendants would receive the gospel and bear the priesthood, and through the ministry of his seed all families of the earth would be blessed, even with the blessings of the gospel, which are the blessings of salvation, even of life eternal. He was blessed with land, promised lands of inheritance too.

Now, he never received these things in his life, and so it's interesting in the process of going through those tests Abraham put the Lord in a very peculiar position. When you do what the Lord says in a covenant situation, and you follow him with exactness, you *bind* the Lord. This is a doctrine that may not be widely understood. You can almost, I hate to use these words, "force the Lord's hand" to give you the blessings that He promised you. And because of Abraham's faithfulness, the Lord still stands to honor the Covenant that was made with Abraham. It is not complete. There's more that needs to be done as Julie just alluded to a minute ago.

So in trying to honor that Covenant, ever since Abraham died, the Lord has tried to establish that Covenant nation that Abraham wanted so desperately. He tried to do it with the Israelites hundreds of years later. Right? I'm just going to kind of glaze through the next few scenes, but think of the Israelites. Moses comes along. He establishes the law. Covenants are made. Rituals begin. But it's all a lower law. And Moses did his best to try to elevate the Israelites to get them to receive these higher ordinances and blessings. Through hard-heartedness and so forth it wasn't realized.

King David came along. He tried to establish a covenant. He didn't do too bad of a job uniting Israel, but it didn't take long before some impure traditions had crept into the Israelite society and before long, Isaiah comes along. He warns, destruction awaits if we don't repent and become that city and nation that Abraham wanted. And so the point here is the Lord really did his best with the Israelites and they completely bombed it. And we read all about this. This was the theme of Isaiah and the scriptures, and many other prophets too. It was a great detriment to these prophets that Israel couldn't establish those covenants that Abraham so desperately wanted for their people.

Now shortly after Isaiah gave those warnings to the Israelites and the Jews in Jerusalem of the time of the impending destruction, we have another prophet arrive on scene, and that's one more familiar to Latter-day Saints; this was Lehi. We all know, in 1st Nephi, chapter 1 of the Book of Mormon, we read how Lehi was a prophet, among many other prophets, who was also sent to warn and prepare the people of impending destruction if they didn't repent. This was the beginning of a new covenant line here. The Lord, in His wisdom, saw fit to call out some of His chosen people among the covenant people, to go to a place of safety, and we can follow this story all the way across the ocean to the Americas. And there are a couple of interesting points that I want to make with regard to the Book of Mormon and the Abrahamic Covenant.

One of the first points being in about 1st Nephi chapter 12, we read about Nephi having his visionary experiences of the future. And no small part of that is the Abrahamic Covenant. If you read through those visionary experiences you read about the angel who takes Nephi on a mountain and they're having questions. Nephi's seeing the mother of the Son of God, Mary, and then you'll see these interesting little questions that the angel who's guiding him along, all of a sudden will say, "Do you remember the covenant of your fathers?" And Nephi would say, "Yes." And then the angel just continues the vision where he was. And then he'll do it again, "Do you remember the covenants of the father's?" Nephi says, "Yes."

It's interesting that this was an important topic and this was an important theme that the Lord wanted Nephi to continually remember these covenants that they experienced. It was obviously impressing upon Nephi's mind the importance of the Abrahamic Covenant and the covenants with Israel. So that was the first point I want to make.

Now if we fast forward another 600 years, another point I want to make about the Abrahamic Covenant is regarding the Savior, Jesus Christ, when he visited the Nephites and the Lamanites shortly after His crucifixion in Jerusalem. There were a lot of reasons the Lord came and appeared to these people, and that's manifest in the account. He blessed children, he administered the Sacrament, he taught the ordinances of baptism, but perhaps the most important reason He came, and He states this, if we go to let me check my notes here, if you go to 3rd Nephi 16:10, the Savior tells the people that He was commanded of the Father to come and speak to them about the

Lord's covenants with Israel. Okay, so this is a bigger big part of the Abrahamic Covenant.

He goes on and He's teaching about these covenants that were established and the purpose of them, and then you know you all remember this part where He says, "I perceive that ye are weak and that you are not able to understand my words." How many of us are like this? When we study the Covenant, sometimes we get a little overwhelmed and maybe don't understand the meaning or the significance of it. But He goes on to say, well go home, pray, fast, study these words, ponder my words, gain light and wisdom, and then I'll come back tomorrow and then we can finish. And so that's the charge He gives the people. But first He blesses their children and they have a Sacrament ceremony.

He comes on the morrow. He begins with a Sacrament ceremony once again. These events are taking place just to elevate their righteousness and spirituality and to help open their minds to receive the rest of the message that He was commanded of the Father to speak. All that took place in the next four chapters, and then suddenly in 3rd Nephi 20: 10, He says, "Now I commence or I continue the message that I was commanded of my Father to give to you." So I just think it's really important to understand while the Savior did a lot of significant things with the ancient Americans, the biggest part of His purpose was to come there and teach the Abrahamic Covenant.

This was the was the message the Father commanded him to give. Christ then witnesses of Isaiah, who spoke of this perhaps more than any other biblical prophet. And then said, "Great are the words of Isaiah." And then He gave us a commandment to study the words of Isaiah. Why would he do that? Again, because Isaiah has probably talked about the Abrahamic Covenant more than anyone else.

Julie: Thank you, Eric.

Eric: So now we have another shot. Okay fast-forward to the 1800s. Here we have the restoration of the gospel. The Lord again remembering His Covenant with Abraham, did his best to re-establish the Kingdom on the earth that would build translated cities of light, righteousness, fullness of the everlasting gospel, fullness of the priesthood ordinances and all the blessings of Salvation. You can read in Doctrine and Covenants how essentially those early Saints kind of blew it. These Saints move west. We establish Salt Lake City out here. Well here we are. We're still under the same obligation to establish this holy nation and I'm going to leave it to each of you to determine how well we're doing at establishing that nation and establishing this Covenant that was made with Abraham.

Okay, so we have this great missionary work and all kinds of things. We've been at it for a hundred and eighty years plus, trying to get people in, to make these covenants, bring them to the temple, and establish all the things that Abraham wanted. So we have Elijah who's come in this dispensation and Abrahamic promises and blessings were promised through Elijah in restoring some of those things. The scripture that says "to turn the hearts of the children to the father's and the hearts of the father's to the children" has everything to do with the Abrahamic Covenant and providing ordinances of exaltation.

That's where we are currently. So now we have this gap between here and the righteous nation that Abraham so desperately wanted, and the Covenant that the Lord made with him to fulfill in these latter days. This is where I now see warners, messengers like Julie coming in and witnessing of how glorious things will be following the days of tribulation. And so with that, Julie, I have covered everything that I wanted to say and turn it to you to say anything you'd like concerning the fulfillment of the Abrahamic Covenant as you see it in the future.

Julie: Thank you, Eric. I just wanted to thank you for the research you've done and for the scriptures you brought to our attention, and to remind us of what's gone on in history.

It's always amazing to me to hear from someone else the wisdom and knowledge they're given through the Spirit, as it confirms my own witness in my own heart what I know to be true. I want to witness and testify of the Abrahamic Covenant that was made with God and Abraham, then and now, that will yet be fulfilled in completeness. I witness and testify that we will yet see this come forth during the tribulations, expanding into the Millennium as we see thousands and thousands of cities of light expand across the world.

I believe that this Abrahamic Covenant also is talking about more than just this world. It's actually talking about beings in the galaxies with Abraham being promised that he will create worlds without number, as we talk about the gathering; as we talk about the covenants that he made with Father to be able to expand in his powers and creations, as he fulfills all righteousness. I believe that this is something that's possible for each and every one of us as we keep our Abrahamic Covenants and as we pass our Abrahamic tests. We can then progress in lights, powers and priesthoods now and beyond the veil. I believe that we have the opportunity to gain light and knowledge here on this earth and on the other side of the veil as we continue to learn what the Lord would have us learn, as we work together as a unified body of those who are followers of Christ in fulfillment of this Covenant.

I understand that we have a great responsibility ahead of us in the coming days as we know that the tribulations are soon upon us. Within the years of tribulations, the Church of the Firstborn will come forth; therefore, providing an opportunity for advanced powers and priesthoods upon the earth to come to fulfillment, fulfilling in portion the Abrahamic Covenant. I understand that with this comes great responsibility for those who are listening within the sound of my voice, as we prepare for the Battle of Armageddon. And with this I leave my witness and testimony with you, letting you know that I know that Abraham is our father who has covenanted with the Father to be able to help us fulfill all righteousness as we gather the children home. I leave this witness with you in the name of Jesus Christ. Amen.

Eric: Thanks Julie. I'm just going to add my quick witness, as well, which comes from the title page of The Book of Mormon where it's discussing the purpose of the Book of Mormon and so forth. It says: "...which is to show unto the remnant of the house of Israel what great things the Lord hath done for their fathers and that they may know the covenants of the Lord." And then I emphasize this next line, "That they are not cast off forever."

So for anyone who's hearing and listening to this, if you are a descendant of Abraham or are adopted into his posterity as a covenant member of the kingdom, you are not cast off forever. Even if you are concerned about the Days of Tribulation, the Lord will remember us in our trials. He will protect us and we will see some of the greatest miracles that have ever been seen if we're faithful. We are not cast off, and I bear testimony that Abraham is our father and that Heavenly Father's Covenant with Abraham is not yet fulfilled. It is upon us in the latter-days to help establish and fulfill that Covenant and restore these cities and righteous nations of cities of light that have been described by Julie and others. And that's my witness in the name of Jesus Christ as well. Thanks Julie.

Julie: Thank you Eric. Until next time, I hope you all are able to find the light and knowledge the Lord would have you receive at this time and that you find peace and calm in your heart as you seek the Lord, and you get answers to your prayers. I leave this with you in his name. Until next time.

My Witness
of Jesus Christ

Julie: Hi, welcome to the Julie Rowe Show. Today is Monday, September 18, 2017. I'm here with Eric Smith and we're getting ready to do another podcast. Eric, thanks for joining us today.

Eric: Thanks Julie. As Julie was just relaying to me, she wanted to talk about the Savior. We've talked about Him a couple of times before but the point of this is to have a little more personal conversation concerning what Julie has seen of Him and her witness of Him personally.

Julie: Right, so basically I just wanted to talk a little bit about what I know of him; what I remember of him; what I feel about him; what I understand about him; his messianic role as well as really just his personality and his nature; his divine nature and we'll just see where this goes. I'm just going to try to speak from my heart and hopefully help some of you who are listening better understand who it is that I call Master.

My heart's really full today, it's been a busy day, it's been a really good day, but I've had some circumstances today that have brought to my memory especially with September 23rd coming up this weekend and it being the anniversary of my near-death experience coming up next week, I guess you could say the stars are aligning for my mission to take hold, and this has weighed on me very heavily but every time it gets heavy I try to turn to the Lord and

He lightens my burden. Now I know most of you don't really know what I'm talking about or why I would feel weighed down or really what my mission is and that's not what the purpose of this podcast is today so I'm not going to go into that but I just want to witness and testify to you that I know that the Lord can open and heal your heart.

I know that he is an all-powerful God who loves you and who misses you and he wants to hear from you. I know that God the Father has created us in his image and we have divine origin. There are so many things I would love to expound on, being able to expound on the scriptures and other doctrines that I just don't have permission to go into but I do know that in simplest terms what it boils down to is the love of Father in Heaven and our elder brother Jesus Christ who would do anything for us; they have done it all for us. They're not asking us to do anything that they themselves have not done. Christ descended below all things; he did this for us.

I know by nature that as a fallen people we have a lack of understanding of who our savior is and we don't remember Him completely but for me it's a little bit different. I don't mean to place myself above anyone, that's not my intention, but I am to serve as a witness of my Savior and my personal relationship with Him and memories that I have of Him. He has an amazing heart, like no other heart I've ever felt. He is a man of His word. He is a man who honors his priesthood power and with that he's been entrusted by the Father. He is a man of Honor of dignity. He is a man of truth. He is a man of hope and, he is a man of love beyond measure, and I miss him.

He has an amazing sense of humor. He can cry with the best of them and he can laugh with them too. He has an embrace like no other I've ever felt. He motivates me to be better. He's healed my heart thousands of times; more times than I can tell you, then and now. He walks in faith and in action. He walks in similitude; he walks in strength. He has the most beautiful hands I've ever seen; his hands pierced; his side pierced; his feet pierced. The blood and sins of this world stained in his memory. Knowingly, he came to this Earth to descend so that man might be and they might return to a loving Father in Heaven that he loves equally.

He loves completely without condition. He loves wholly for the purpose of serving his God and his Father and all of his brothers and sisters. He is without guile. He is a God of love, a God of humility, and the Son of the living God. He walks with powers in his footsteps, strength in his sinews, and power in the priesthood. He seeks the Father's will. He commands the elements. He dictates through his heart and with that he rules and reigns with dignity, power, purpose, and love.

The nature of God is hard to explain to someone who can't remember him; but in my heart there is a longing to return home to the God that I know, to a brother who is always happy to see me and helps me seek refuge from this world that I live in and teaches me how to be a better woman.

My prayer is that I can one day stand with him, as his friend, gathering the children back to our Father. My hope is that I can live worthy to look in his face, feel his embrace, and join with him with our Father in gathering the family and healing the family. My hope is that I can be a woman worthy of the love that my Father has bestowed upon me and that without condition I will stand as an honorable daughter of God ready to meet my maker.

I leave this prayer with you testifying and witnessing of God's eternal nature; of his eternal love and his infinite atonement which is for all mankind. Men, women, and children, wherever they may be within the sound of my voice, I witness and testify to you that God in his very nature is the most whole being I've ever met; and with that I stand ready to be his witness, his friend, and his servant. I leave this witness with you, and pray that you will each find your strength, your role, your mission and your divine worth as you seek the God who loves you so much. And I leave this witness and testimony with you in Christ's name. Amen.

Eric: Thank you Julie

Prophets and Prophecy

Episode 40

Julie: Welcome to the Julie Rowe Show. Today is Tuesday, September 19, 2017. Eric, welcome to the show. Would you like to introduce our topic for us?

Eric: Sure. Thanks Julie. And thanks to everybody who's tuning in. We've had tremendous support. We are getting wonderful feedback through email and comments on podcasts and so forth. We're grateful for you guys and we're humbled to know that these podcasts are helping and instructing and edifying people. So, thank you again for tuning in.

I got real serious about this topic after I read Julie's books and some other near-death experience books. It's regarding the spirit of prophecy and prophets. You know as I read about Julie's experience, I began to see that what in effect Julie was doing was prophesying of things to come, which led to questions about prophecy. Who is entitled to prophesy and the channels prophecy should come through and should not come through. Her book really launched me on an incredible doctrinal journey.

I've learned a lot of things along the way, and I know many of you listening have as well, but I'd like to share some of those findings with you. As always, Julie, this will be kind of heavy on the doctrinal side, so please chime in as the Spirit directs. Your witness always helps bring life to the subjects.

Julie: Great. Thanks Eric.

Eric: You bet. Okay, so I think a nice place to start on this topic is back in Numbers 11:28. Here we have the experience of the Israelites. Actually I might start at verse 26:

> "But there remained two of the men in camp. The name of the one was Eldad, and the other was Medad: and the spirit rested upon them; and they were of them that were written, but went not out unto the tabernacle: and they prophesied in the camp. And there ran a young man, and told Moses, and said, Eldad and Medad do prophesy in the camp. And Joshua the son of Nun, the servant of Moses, one of his young men, answered and said, My Lord Moses, forbid them. And Moses said unto Him, enviest thou for my sake? Would God that all the Lord's people were prophets, and that the Lord would put his spirit upon them!"

We've shared this before, but in effect what was happening is the people thought prophecy should only come from Moses, and they were essentially tattle-telling on these other two people who had the spirit of prophecy. Moses adds his witness that the spirit of prophecy is good. It's not reserved for certain people. And that he wished that all people had those gifts to be able to prophesy.

Now there are numerous accounts in scripture where there were people who had the spirit of prophecy among them, and I want to go through a lot of these, which include the New Testament, the Old Testament, and the Book of Mormon. We have experiences of people prophesying in these latter days, in the early days of the restoration, and so I want to drill this point home because in our culture in the church today, there are some views that prophecy should only be held by certain people and who get a little uncomfortable anytime other people prophesy, and so I'd like to put that to rest - and it's easy to do doctrinally and scripturally.

Another place we can turn is Jacob 4:6 and 13 in the Book of Mormon, where Jacob says:

"Wherefore, we search the prophets, and we have many revelations and the spirit of prophecy; and having all these witnesses we obtain a hope, and our faith becometh unshaken. Behold, my brethren, he that prophesieth, let him prophesy to the understanding of men; for the Spirit speaketh the truth and lieth not. Wherefore, it speaketh of things as they really are, and of things as they really will be; wherefore, these things are manifested unto us plainly, for the salvation of our souls. But behold, we are not witnesses alone in these things; for God also spake them unto prophets of old."

So the spirit of prophecy was held among the days of Nephi and Jacob. There are other biblical stories that talk about the spirit of prophecy; some of which are difficult for us to reconcile. I think of the prophet Jonah, for example. Jonah has a little bit of a bad rap for not being the most faithful or the most diligent. He was a little sluggish in his willingness to go and prophesy to the people and to warn them. There are reasons for this. If we compare him to Joseph Smith, Abraham, or Brigham Young, he was a little more resistant.

We have talked in another podcast or two about the way ancient Israel was governed. To recap that again very briefly, to an Israelite in ancient times they would have looked to three sources for direction: the king or the civic leader (I say civic leader because they also had judges and other forms of government); they would have looked to the priests who oversaw temple rites, rituals, and ordinances; and they would have looked to anyone from the third group of government they would have called prophets, warners, teachers or messengers. Jonah would have fit in this third category of someone who held the spirit of prophecy, who was called of God to warn and testify and teach.

There are a number of examples like that, and there are many women who fall in this category. Again, a lot of times now days we don't quite know what to do with people like Miriam, Deborah, Hulda, Anna, or even the mother of the Savior, Mary, who was known to have had the gift and spirit of prophecy. And so what do we do with these women? Well, they fit in this third category of warners, messengers, teachers, prophets; those who had the spirit of prophecy.

The idea that women had prophetic gifts in those days not only feels right to me, but is doctrinal. So consider the words of Alma in the Book of Mormon when he spoke of those who had spiritual gifts. He said: "*And now, he imparteth his word by angels unto men, yea, not only men but women also. Now this not all; little children do have words given unto them many times, which confound the wise and the learned.*" That's Alma 32:23. Alma was trying to make the case that prophecy is not limited, and that the Lord does not limit the spirit and gift of prophecy to certain people.

And lastly in this little subcategory here, the Prophet Joel in the Old Testament in Chapter 2:28, he clearly distinguishes between different categories of people as well. He says, "*your sons and your daughters shall prophesy, your old men shall dream dreams, your young men shall see visions*". So Joel trying to make the case that the Lord does not limit those who have the spirit of prophecy. Julie on that note, I've been talking a lot, do you have anything that's come to your mind so far?

Julie: Well I just appreciate what you said and how you've started to lay out the doctrine for us. It's important that we understand the doctrine before we can understand certain gospel principles that come in line with the doctrine. When we understand doctrine, we have a clearer picture of who we are as divine sons and daughters of God, and who others are. We have an understanding of the purpose of why we're here and where we're going and why we're doing this mortal probation that we're on. So I appreciate you laying the foundation of the doctrine.

There have been a lot of people in the last three years that have had a problem with what I'm doing or what I'm sharing. I want to witness and testify that I know without a doubt, with a hundred percent surety that the Lord has given me the assignment to share my story and to share my visions and to share my near-death experience, and to share the gifts that the Lord has given me. I don't share all of them but I do share the gift that He has given me regarding the future visions on America and some of the past things I've seen. There are higher purposes in this that I'm not going to disclose at this time, and one day, when the veil is gone for everyone, you guys will understand more why I know this.

I do need to witness and testify that I have a sure knowledge of this now, and that I do know that I'm on assignment from the Lord to share these prophecies. And I have not wanted to own that message as boldly as I feel like I need to today. In fact, when Eric presented this topic to me a month or two ago, I told him I just wasn't comfortable with that; that I don't want people calling me a *prophet* or *prophetess*. I told him if I do that they're going to stone me. We know what happens when you are called a prophet or prophetess. It never goes well, and I have never called myself that.

The Lord has been telling me, "Julie, you need to own the message. You need to own your mission and don't shy away from it." And so I appreciate you, Eric, for giving me the courage today to go public with more of what I experienced, and to stand tall and to stand encouraged that the Lord has in fact has given me these gifts; and I'm not supposed to shy away from owning that.

The role that I have is significant to be able to help prepare people for the days that are coming. I trust that the Lord will prepare the hearts of the children. What I mean by that is all of us, as brothers and sisters, that the Lord will prepare our hearts to receive whatever message that Eric shares today. I trust the Lord, and I don't know what that message is, you guys. He shared a little bit with me a month or so ago and I kind of did one of these like yeah, yeah, yeah, I don't want to hear that. And then the Lord softened my heart last week and said, "Julie, it's time." And then on Saturday I was shown some more things in vision about who I am and more of the mission, and the Lord said, "Julie it's time. You need to have Eric do this podcast. He was inspired when he came up with this. Don't stand in his way." And so that is why we're doing the podcast today.

Eric: Interesting. I always like that background information. I get these hunches and impressions that we should do things, and kind of wonder, "Am I being led by the spirit, or is this just kind of my own will?", you know. And so I'm grateful for that feedback, Julie. Thanks.

Julie: Yeah.

Eric: Even with what's been said here, I can hear in my mind's ear and in my mind's eye, I can see people saying, "Did you hear what she said? Do you hear what they're saying right now? They're saying she's a prophet!" To anyone who struggles with this message I will call you out on it and say you do not understand the doctrine! Study the scriptures. This is plain, basic information and has been understood for centuries. Only in recent times has this doctrine been misunderstood and forgotten.

I want to illustrate this further. Dallin H. Oaks is a modern apostle of the Lord Jesus Christ. I believe in him and I sustain him, and I hold him as a Prophet, Seer and Revelator. He is known to have said in his wonderful talk called, *Spiritual Gifts*: "*It is important for us to understand the distinction between a prophet, who has the spiritual gift of prophecy, and the prophet, who has the prophetic office.*" He went on to explain that, "*When we hear the word prophet in our day, we are accustomed to thinking of the prophet. These words signify him who holds the prophetic office and is sustained as the prophet, seer, and revelator. The priesthood offices and powers exercised by the President of the Church are unique.*" And I testify that what he's saying there is true. He goes on to say:

"As we read in the Book of Revelation, 'The testimony of Jesus is the spirit of prophecy.' The Prophet Joseph Smith relied on this scripture in teaching that 'every other man who has the testimony of Jesus' is a prophet. Similarly, the Apostle Paul stated that 'he that prophesieth speaketh unto men to edification, and exhortation, and comfort.' Thus, in the sense used in speaking of spiritual gifts, a prophet is one who testifies of Jesus Christ, teaches God's word, and exhorts God's people. In its scriptural sense, to prophesy means much more than to predict the future."

Okay, so that was given in 1986, Dallin H. Oaks, making a distinction between prophets who 'hold the prophetic office' and 'prophets who have the spiritual gift of prophesy.' From here on forward I'm going to say prophet with a big 'P' is one who holds the prophetic office, and prophet with a little 'p' is one who has the prophetic gifts of the Spirit that Dallin H. Oaks talked about.

We have examples of both throughout the scriptures. Just as a quick example of prophets with a little 'p' is Lehi in the Book of Mormon; you can read about that in the first chapter; Nephi, his son, is sort of an example of that; Samuel the Lamanite. And then there are a number of other prophets with little 'p's that we just don't have the names of. There are many in the New Testament, Old Testament, and many in the Book of Mormon as well.

I want to turn to the LDS Topical Guide and encourage you to look up *Prophecy*, which I'm going to read here: "*A prophecy may pertain to the past, present or future. When a person prophecies he speaks or writes that which God wants Him to know for his own good*" and then I emphasize this next part, "*or the good of others.*" This is a distinction we don't talk about. I don't think we understand collectively what it means in the Church. According to this, you can, and are entitled to receive prophecy for yourself *and for others.* Now I know that makes people uncomfortable because it's been pounded and pounded in our minds and over the pulpit that you can't receive revelation for other people.

I don't know about that doctrine. It feels a little incomplete. I know that we *can* receive revelation for others, but I think there's a distinction we have to be careful about. To *command* others is really where I think we need to be careful. If Julie, Chad Daybell, Jonathan Cahn, or any number of other prophets with the little 'p' were to tell me that I needed to do something, I would immediately cast them out and say you are out of line, you don't have the authority to tell me what to do. Now, I do believe these people have seen things in the future. I know Julie has seen what she says she's seen. I knew that the moment I read her book. I have never heard Julie say that I should do something because of what she's seen, and if she did that would be a big red flag to me.

So again, that's in the LDS Topical Guide. Look it up. It's under 'Prophecy', and makes it pretty clear that it is possible for you to receive prophetic insight on behalf of others. I think by extension that means you could share your revelation with them if the Spirit directs you, but that does not give you the right to command them or give them instruction in behalf of what you've seen. Any thoughts there Julie?

Julie: I just agree with you. I want a state for the official record that I never have told anyone - of those that I've had revelation about - I've been very, very careful to make sure that I respect agency. The Spirit's very firm with me in what I'm allowed to say regarding someone's mission or someone's life. If I'm shown future scenes of them, I don't share it. If they ask questions I can witness and confirm but generally speaking, I do not initiate it other than what you've heard me write in my books or say on the podcasts.

On an individual basis the pattern is that people come to me, and if I have permission from the Spirit, then I can confirm the witness what the revelation has been given to them, even if I've already been given that revelation. That's important because it's easy for us to get deceived and to overstep the bounds the Lord has given us. Once revelation is given, it penetrates the heart when it comes from the Holy Ghost versus another person. Or if I'm speaking as a prophetess first per se as I'm speaking words of truth through the gift of prophecy and I share something with someone that they're not quite ready to hear yet or they're not ready to accept into their heart as truth, then it can kind of cause a stumbling block. And so it's important that we listen to the Spirit and pattern our behavior after the way that the Lord has His pattern which is to be very careful about how we say things, when we say things, and doing the best we can to discern.

This is something that's a constant juggling act for me because I recognize that as I share things, people's eyes, ears, and hearts are opened up to possibilities; it opens up their eyes, ears, and hearts to the possibility of who they are, where they come from, and where they're going in the eternal perspective as well as here on earth. I don't want to be the one accountable for opening someone's eyes when essentially they weren't ready. All the Lord tells me is that they wouldn't be opened if they weren't ready anyway. So there's kind of a little catch-22 there with me trying to understand my mission and how things fall into play when it comes to discerning what I can and can't say.

Additionally, I would be very cautious if upon meeting someone they receive revelation for you and told you what to do. There are individuals that have been given information about me and they have served as witnesses to me after I've been given that revelation. There have been a couple situations in the last month or two where I've met individuals who are very spiritually gifted and had been given revelation about me, and in one case I can think of they were given the wrong information. I was given information about myself that I knew to be true. They were given some of it and then they kind of filled in the blanks with their own understanding or they had a false spirit that told them the rest of the message, which can be a very dangerous thing, when people are not able to discern truth and imparting what they think is truth onto another individual.

So I just want to give a word of caution, as your gifts increase, be very discerning with and making sure that you know it's in fact, the Holy Ghost who has penetrated your heart; that it really is the Spirit speaking to you, and that it's not a false spirit or an unclean spirit or someone who is just, I mean, the spirits on the other side of the veil, as the veil gets thin, are getting more and more crafty in mimicking the voices, the energy, the thought patterns, and the energy of angels of light. They will come, pretending to be angels of light, when in fact they are just deceivers. And so I'm always looking for additional witnesses on the other side of the veil before I speak. And I'm always looking for witnesses on this side of the veil. The Lord works through the law of witnesses.

Eric: Very well said, Julie. Thank you for that. And it's a really good segue into the next bullet point that I wanted to discuss - this idea of discerning between the voices that come at us.

Why do we have the need to discern in the first place? Why did the Savior mention this? When we read the New Testament, we read about Jesus Christ teaching the way to discern between a sheep and one who's a ravening wolf and who is basically dressed in sheep's clothing. Why did the Savior teach that? Why did He even teach us to distinguish between true and false prophets?

In a contemporary, cultural perspective, we see that there is only one need to listen to one prophet, and so we don't look elsewhere for instruction. So again, if the Lord were to have spoken that in His day in our cultural, contemporary view, He would have said: *just follow Peter when I'm gone, He knows the way.* He didn't say that. He taught us to look for the signs to detect a wolf from a sheep and to know the difference. His council was really, really simple: *by their fruits ye shall know them.* And so he's saying that you study the person's life and what they're like.

I'm aware of people who claim to be prophets out there on a Sunday or something, and then during the week, they do adulterous things. Or they seem to not practice what they preach and stuff. So it's kind of obvious sometimes when there's a wolf in sheep's clothing. But again it's by their fruits ye shall know them. Just look at the person's fruits and the Savior's doctrine here really is simple. I think by extension of Him teaching this and trying to delineate between following a true and false prophet, I believe He was also sort of saying you *should* be watching for true prophets. You *should* be watching for those who have a true message, because they can help you along the way and they can help you see things that maybe you wouldn't have seen otherwise.

Joseph Smith stated concerning this idea of false prophets: "False prophets always arise to oppose the true prophets" (Teachings of the Prophet, page 365). It's another test we can use when filtering to know if the message is from somebody of the light or somebody of the dark. This is important. It hasn't been that important in the last 150 years because we've had the leaders right before our eyes and it's easy. I think what's happened in the last hundred and eighty years is we had those who have the spiritual gift of prophecy and who hold the prophetic office right before our eyes, so it's easy to say "just follow them, and then I don't really even have to think or question if there's anybody else to follow."

I think also we don't even really question some of the things our own leaders say because they're in that category. It is important for us to always filter, even with those who are called, and Brigham Young supports this idea. Never, never just take for granted what a prophet of the Lord is saying. You should always pray and get your own witness. Any thoughts there Julie?

Julie: I just think it's important that we continually draw upon the Lord for inspiration and we go to Him to get a confirmation of doctrines and principles and laws of the gospel. When we take it to the Lord, then the Holy Ghost witnesses to our heart, it penetrates our heart, and there's no mistaking when you get a confirmation from the Spirit. Therefore, no matter what it is you're called upon to do once you've had confirmation, you can press forward in faith without fear.

It's when we don't have confirmations of doctrines, when we don't have confirmations of principles, we don't have confirmations of laws of the gospel, that the adversary is able to come in and thwart our progress because he sends his lying and deceiving false doctrines, his false teachings, false belief systems, and false traditions to get in the way and impede our progress. I can't emphasize enough the importance of taking our questions to the Lord; waiting upon the Lord; asking for confirmation; and being patient till we get it. And then once we get it, acting in faith so that we can one day have a sure knowledge of what it is we're being taught.

Eric: I want to ask you another question, Julie. This isn't planned, but I was just talking about the Savior delineating between true and false prophets, and I believe that was wise counsel for our day. I have this feeling that in the future there will rise more true and false prophets. In other words, we're going to start getting messages from all kinds of people, and some of those messages, I presume, will be of the light, and I think some will be of the dark. Do you have any thoughts or insight on that?

Julie: Yes. All you have to do is search on the Internet and you'll find there's lots of people claiming prophetic gifts. Now I don't doubt that they're seeing things or they're being told things; the question is, what is their source? Is it coming from the light, or the dark? It's very important that we learn to discern the voices on both sides of the veil. The only way you can do that is to take charge of your heart. Take your heart to the Lord. Ask him with complete faith and trust that he'll give you the answer to know whether or not that's a true messenger.

There are a lot of good people on this planet that have prophetic gifts, and they're not of the LDS faith, and they are prophets and prophetesses. They have just as much of a gift but they are also just as vulnerable as we are, if not more so, because most of them don't have the doctrines to fall back on. So we need to be very careful who we listen to, but draw upon the law of witnesses; the Lord is giving many, many witnesses of the days that we're in.

I foresee, as it's been prophesied in scripture, that there will be an increase in false prophets, and an increase in true prophecy. This has been spoken of by prophets of all ages. This is going to happen. We're living in the very last of the last days, and I know this to be true. I have a sure witness and a sure knowledge that we are going to see this in very short order.

I guarantee you the minute that Wasatch Earthquake happens there are going to be all kinds of people come out of the woodwork trying to claim that they knew, just like Julie Rowe, when that earthquake was going to happen. And then they're going to be in lying wait to try to deceive people and other things. And they would be servants of the devil, because people will not be able to discern the difference between who to listen to and who not to listen to.

Eric: Very interesting. I want to add to that, in watching between true and false prophets and prophecies coming forth. Also we shouldn't be idle and casual about saying, "Well I'm not going to listen to any of them. I'm just going to follow one." That's good, and I'm speaking of the Prophet of the LDS Church, but I'm saying, always listen to him; no question; absolutely; for sure; guaranteed every time; But don't limit yourself to him either. There will be others who have information that can be useful to you. We shouldn't be idle and just casual in who we listen to. We should be very eager and engaged in all the things that are coming our way.

Julie: I appreciate you saying that. Again this goes to the importance of working in councils. It goes to the importance of why things are patterned the way they are in the heavens and on this earth. The Prophet has the First Presidency and the Quorum of the Twelve. They work, in part, as a quorum because they are a council and a law of witnesses. When we watch General Conference we don't listen to just one talk and one guy speak, we listen to men and women who are inspired of God that have prophetic callings, and I witness and testify of that. Working in councils is the divine order of the of the universe.

Also, we work in the law of witnesses. When you have two or more witnesses, you know the truth of all things, through the law of witnesses. And in those very, very important things you can have more than two witnesses. You'll have three or four or five, if not fifteen or twenty witnesses of a certain doctrine or a certain fact or a certain truth. And where it's important, the Lord will give you that witness. You need to study it. You need to wrestle with the Lord on it. And then, when it's time for you in your plan to understand the doctrine, He will give you that sure knowledge, just like He's given it to me.

Eric: Very good. Thank you. I have a final thought here, just this scriptural pattern of *prophets*, in the plural sense. I've addressed this before but it's worth mentioning again. In 1st Nephi 1:4 it says: "*And there came prophets in the land again, crying repentance unto them--that they must prepare the way of the Lord or there should come a curse upon the face of land; yea, even there should be a great famine in which they should be destroyed if they did not repent*" (Ether 9:28).

We learn a lot in that verse. First of all, that there are *prophets* in the plural sense, coming in, moved upon by the Spirit of the Lord, to cry repentance unto people. And why? Usually, because destruction lies upon the door and because of the sins of the generation.

There's no question in my mind that we live in a similar day when destruction awaits because of our sins; because of the collective sins of this generation, and there's evil all over the face of the earth. We can't really dispute that; and certainly the destruction that awaits us is very scriptural. It's discussed frequently throughout the scriptures. It's known as The Days of Tribulation, The Day of Sorrow. We've talked about this before; it is a very scriptural concept. And so it would only make sense that the Lord is sending additional prophets and warners again, because of the impending destruction.

Jarom 1:4 is another place where it says: "*And there are many among us who have many revelations, for they are not all stiffnecked.*" Now that doesn't say prophets, but it does say there *were many* who received revelations.

In Enos 1:22: "*And there were exceedingly many prophets among us. And the people were a stiffnecked people, hard to understand.*" Why? So we had *many prophets* among the people who were stiffnecked and hard-hearted.

3rd Nephi 3:19 says: "*Now it was the custom*" - I love this one! I think it's really interesting to see, in times of war, how Nephites and Israelites would call upon someone who had the spirit of prophecy to give them that competitive edge against the enemy. Here it says: "*Now it was the custom among all the Nephites to appoint for their chief captains, (save it were in their times of wickedness) someone that had the spirit of revelation and also prophecy; therefore, this Gidgiddoni was a great prophet among them, as also was the chief judge.*"

We read in the book of Ether, in four different places, where it used the phrase *many prophets*; there were many prophets who came among them just before times of destruction, in times of war. And so the Lord, in His mercy, saw fit to send many prophets to warn those people.

There's another thought that I just I didn't know where else to say it but right here. If the people in the times we live in repented and were a righteous people and not a stiff-necked people, and if we were all harkening and listening to the prophet and those who work with him, I know that people like Julie and Chad and all these others who have these prophetic gifts would be at home with their families; living their lives in peace and happiness. There would be no need for them to rise like they have. There would have been no need for them to necessarily have all these visions of calamities in future times because there may not be calamities in future times if we were all living righteously.

So, in that sense, I sympathize with people like Julie who on a daily basis can't really live what we might call a "normal life." For all intents and purposes, she should be home with her family right now;

we shouldn't be doing this podcast; She should be having ice cream and helping her kids do homework, and doing those sorts of things. And that's kind of my final remark. I have a little concluding witness I'd like to say here in a minute. But Julie, do you have anything you'd like to add to that first?

Julie: Yeah. I just wanted to thank you for your time, Eric, and for everyone for listening today. I'd like to add my witness and let you know that I'm very, very happy to be doing these podcasts; very, very happy to be doing my mission. I have never been happier in my life than I am right now, because the Lord is giving me a fullness of joy and he's answering my prayers.

I have had numerous prayers answered about my identity, about my mission, about who I am, where I came from, and why I'm here. I've had answers to questions I had when I woke up from my near-death experience and the veil was back, and reminder dreams and visions of experiences I had in history past, present, and future. Things are making so much more sense, and so these podcasts serve as a wonderful way to clear energy, to help give me an opportunity to learn more. When questions are asked of me, the veil opens. It answers my questions when I answer yours. And so I just wanted to thank you for the opportunity to work with you Eric.

Eric: Thanks Julie. Likewise, it's a real privilege for me too. I feel so blessed. Just in closing, I just want to re-emphasize that there were prophets of old and in modern times. According to Moses, Paul, Moroni, Joseph Smith, and the Savior Himself, Julie, you are a prophetess! I don't say it with the least degree of hesitation. I don't feel bad saying it. I'm not afraid if people think I'm off my rocker, because it's true.

I want to encourage anyone within the sound of my voice to search your hearts and know it's true. Don't live in fear that the Lord has sent people like Julie to help us understand more. Its scriptural. If there are any within the sound of my voice who would use my words against me to try to cause me to lose my membership in the Church, or my position at work, or whatever; if you have those motives in your heart, you will prove your ignorance in understanding these doctrines.

I call you out on it. I challenge you to study these basic doctrines of the gospel, to pray and fast over them as I have. I have cried over these things. I've taken these things to the temple. I've searched the scriptures diligently to try to understand who the gift of prophecy is able to be given to. I know it's true with all the fiber of my being - every part of my soul.

I witness that this is the Savior's will. This is what Heavenly Father has in mind for us, to give us many opportunities to be warned. I'm so grateful to Him. I know it is evidence that He loves us. He wants to warn us. He's concerned about our salvation. He wants what's best for us. He wants us to make it through The Days of Tribulation. He wants us to turn to Him. He's giving us every opportunity He can. I feel so strongly about this doctrine that I am willing to go to my grave defending it - that the spirit of prophecy is available to all those who will ask, and the spirit of prophecy is alive and well in many people today. And Julie, you are part of that group, and I'm humbled to know you. Thank you.

Julie: Thank you Eric. I just wanted to add my witness and testimony that I know Eric speaks truth. I too will go to my grave. I've seen it. And they who've stoned the prophets before can do the same to me, but that too is part of my mission. I witness and testify that is my truth as I know it. And every bit of it is worth it. I leave this witness and testimony with you in the name of our Savior Jesus Christ. Amen.

OTHER BOOKS

A Greater Tomorrow – *My Journey Beyond the Veil.* By Julie Rowe

The Time is Now. By Julie Rowe

From Tragedy to Destiny. By Julie Rowe

Rising Above the Flames – *My Untold Story.* As told to Eric J. Smith

The Julie Rowe Show – Volume 1. By Julie Rowe and Eric J. Smith

What I See; The Julie Rowe Show, Volume 2.

The Message; The Julie Rowe Show, Volume 3.

Future Volumes in This Series

Out of Darkness Into Light - Volume 5

41: Dates, Signs, Revelations, and NDE's

42: Sadducees and Pharisees

43: Condescension

44: Charity

45: Forgiveness

46: Fortitude

47: Accountability

48: Letting Go of the Outcome

49A: Memories from Julie's Book of Life Part I

49B: Christmas

50: Truth

Memories From the Book of Life - Volume 6

51: Memories from Adam to Jacob

Hidden Bloodlines - Volume 7

THE TRUE SHEPHERD - VOLUME 8

Made in the USA
Monee, IL
24 January 2021